'Inspiring stories, proven principles, and powerful insights all in one amazing book that will change your personal, professional and financial destiny.'
Dr John Demartini, Star of *The Secret* and International Bestselling Author of *The Values Factor: The Secret to Creating an Inspiring and Fulfilling Life*

'Every now and again a book comes along that changes the game. This is one such book. Read it and apply its principles and your levels of fulfilment and personal income will dramatically increase.'
Sháá Wasmund MBE, *Sunday Times* Bestselling Author, *Stop Thinking Start Doing*

'In the information age ordinary people are amassing fortunes and making a positive difference sharing their knowledge and know-how with the world. Your life lessons are valuable and this book will show you how to monetize them.'
Kevin Green, Star of *The Secret Millionaire* *KevinGreen.co.uk*

'This book will seriously increase your ability to **impact**, **inspire**, **influence** and make a much bigger **income**...!'
Raymond Aaron, *New York Times* Bestselling Author

'After implementing Andy's strategies I now have people going crazy for my message and lining up to buy my products and services.'
James Lavers, JamesLavers.com

'Since following the ideas in this book I now make $10,000 to $30,000 per hour sharing my knowledge about social media.'
Paul O'Mahony, PaulOMahony.com

'Applying the tactics taught in this book I pulled in £468,000 in sales from just one single presentation, not bad for someone who previously worked for British Telecom.'
Simon Coulson, InternetBusinessSchool.com

'Before I met Andy Harrington I couldn't even hold a microphone, but now I have been invited to speak and share my knowledge all over the world it's been amazing.'
Mili Ponce, Social Media Expert

'Andy Harrington is the master of communication – he teaches not only what to say but how to say it as well. I launched my own "how to" information product online and made sales of $1,000,000 in just the first 24hrs. The information in this book might just help you do the same.'
Chris Farrell, ChrisFarrell.com

'Andy Harrington is the expert for experts, or those wanting to become experts and share their knowledge and knowhow with the world. This book gives an indispensible guide to carving out a successful career in the lucrative mentoring industry.'
Nick James and Dan Bradbury, BusinessGrowthSystems.co.uk

Andy Harrington is one of the best if not the best in the business at helping you to make a full on career sharing your expertise from the stage. His advice has helped me immensely – in fact last weekend I did two presentations and did over £55,000 in sales.
Rob Moore, ProgressiveProperty.com

I've been in the expert business for over 5 years but only recently my results have been incredible, all because I worked with Andy. His strategies, his coaching, his ideas enabled me to quadruple my results, and gain a 400% increase in business.
Daniel Wagner, Author of *Expert Success*

PASSION INTO PROFIT

How to Make Big Money from Who You Are and What You Know

ANDY HARRINGTON

CAPSTONE
A Wiley Brand

This edition first published 2015

© 2015 Jet Set Speaker Ltd

Registered office

John Wiley and Sons Ltd, The Atrium, Southern Gate, Chichester, West Sussex, PO19 8SQ, United Kingdom

For details of our global editorial offices, for customer services and for information about how to apply for permission to reuse the copyright material in this book please see our website at www.wiley.com.

The right of the author to be identified as the author of this work has been asserted in accordance with the Copyright, Designs and Patents Act 1988.

Reprinted March 2015

Wiley publishes in a variety of print and electronic formats and by print-on-demand. Some material included with standard print versions of this book may not be included in e-books or in print-on-demand. If this book refers to media such as a CD or DVD that is not included in the version you purchased, you may download this material at http://booksupport.wiley.com. For more information about Wiley products, visit www.wiley.com.

Designations used by companies to distinguish their products are often claimed as trademarks. All brand names and product names used in this book and on its cover are trade names, service marks, trademark or registered trademarks of their respective owners. The publisher and the book are not associated with any product or vendor mentioned in this book. None of the companies referenced within the book have endorsed the book.

Limit of Liability/Disclaimer of Warranty: While the publisher and author have used their best efforts in preparing this book, they make no representations or warranties with the respect to the accuracy or completeness of the contents of this book and specifically disclaim any implied warranties of merchantability or fitness for a particular purpose. It is sold on the understanding that the publisher is not engaged in rendering professional services and neither the publisher nor the author shall be liable for damages arising herefrom. If professional advice or other expert assistance is required, the services of a competent professional should be sought.

Library of Congress Cataloging-in-Publication Data is available

A catalogue record for this book is available from the British Library.

ISBN 978-0-857-08616-7 (paperback)

ISBN 978-0-857-08614-3 (ebk) ISBN 978-0-857-08615-0 (ebk)

Cover design: Wiley

Set in 10/13 pt Myriad Pro by Sparks Publishing Services Ltd (www.sparkspublishing.com)

Printed in Great Britain by TJ International Ltd, Padstow, Cornwall, UK

For Beckie

CONTENTS

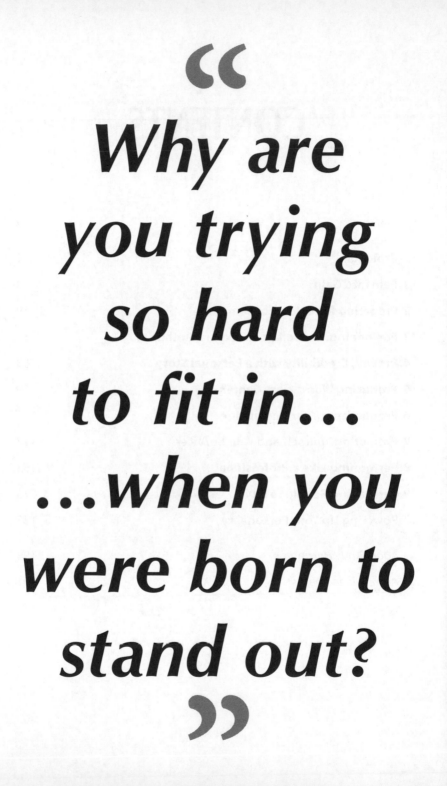

"*Why are you trying so hard to fit in...*
...when you were born to stand out?"

PREFACE

This book is based on nine fundamental truths.

Truth no 1

The knowledge, knowhow and experience you have acquired to date are valuable assets. There are people in the world right now that are willing to pay money to learn how to do what you can already do and know what you already know.

Truth no 2

Everything that has happened in your life, good or bad, has happened for a reason. Your experiences have gifted you a unique empathy with people who face what you faced. Now you are perfectly positioned to give something back to them and be a source of information and inspiration.

Truth no 3

If you have overcome the pain of failure, rejection or loss in your personal or professional life, you will have learned valuable lessons. These lessons can be 'packaged' into helpful advice in the forms of articles, posts, blogs, books, home study programmes, podcasts, online videos, webinars and workshops.

Truth no 4

There are an ever-growing number of advisors, consultants, coaches, therapists, practitioners, mentors, experts, speakers, trainers and seminar leaders who are rapidly transforming from a total unknown to an expert, from an expert to an authority and from an authority to a celebrity in their industry or niche.

Truth no 5

The world has changed. You no longer need to be skilled and experienced and forever allowing an employer to capitalize on that knowledge and wisdom while you get paid a fraction of what they are making out of you.

Truth no 6

You are living in the information age, where it is possible to deliver and sell your knowhow and expertise online, on a stage, or on the small screen of your computer through email, social media and your website.

Truth no 7

You can reach thousands if not millions of people with your advice and 'how to' information, and make thousands if not millions in revenue helping other people to get ahead or overcome a personal or professional problem.

Truth no 8

You don't need to be qualified, certified, or have letters after your name. Your qualifications are your life experiences, your passion for helping others and your determination to make a difference.

Truth no 9

You can do this, even if right now you're not sure how. In this book I will show you step-by-step what to do and how to do it from a standing start.

If any of these truths have resonated with you and if you haven't done so already, please invest in this book and I will reveal to you how to turn a **passion into profit**.

Andy Harrington

But before we begin our journey together, there is something I think you ought to know …

PROLOGUE

It's November 2012 and even though I am standing at the back of the ballroom of the Grosvenor House Hotel, London, it's clear for all to see he's larger than life. I can't believe he's here. I've been waiting for this moment for ten years. I've dreamt about it, and even had nightmares. This is my chance.

I scan the environment. I'm weighing up my options. On the stage is the diminutive comedian Ruby Wax. The stage is flanked on both sides by four US Secret Service agents in their pristine black suits. I chuckle to myself. I can't help thinking that this looks like a scene from a Hollywood blockbuster.

'Ladies and gentlemen.' My momentary lapse of concentration is broken by Ruby Wax's nasal accent. 'Please welcome to the stage the former President of the United States of America, Bill Clinton.'

The 300-strong audience rises to its feet, applauding enthusiastically. But I'm not one of them. My mind is on more important things. Don't get me wrong – I admire Bill Clinton's humanitarian work, but this is my chance to end something that began ten years earlier. If I take my chance, this will be the end of an era.

I take a deep breath to calm my nerves but my self-talk is in overdrive …

'Maybe I should just go home to Beckie and forget this whole thing?' But I quickly chastise myself for even thinking it. 'No, Andy – you've planned for this moment far too long to back out now!'

I'm staring, focused on one guest of honour at the top table, and I resolve that this is the day to do it. All eyes and ears are with Clinton. But not mine.

My mind wanders back to 11 years earlier at the law courts of the Old Bailey in London, where this all started.

CHAPTER 1
PAIN INTO GAIN

It's November 2001. I'm sitting in the viewing gallery of Court No. 4, and if you were sitting next to me you would have been looking down on the old wooden panels and the officious-looking people wearing capes and wigs. I can't help but feel intimidated by the gravitas of the room.

As I look down on the accused, the relative safety of the gallery is shattered as he looks up at us and secretly makes a cut-throat gesture that sends a shiver down my spine.

In the dock is a small, boyish-looking girl in her early 20s with short, dark hair giving evidence. Her chin is on her chest. She's just been cross-examined and it's not gone well. After a few moments that seem like eternity, her own counsel asks her one final question.

'Is there anything you would like to add yourself?'

The young girl grips the rail tighter. She's visibly shaking but there is a determined steeliness to her voice. She looks up and addresses the accused directly.

'I'm going to say something to you now that I didn't have the courage to say before.' There is a hushed silence in the courtroom.

3

'NO!

'No longer am I going to believe it was my fault, no longer am I going to keep your secret. It's over. It doesn't matter what the verdict is – the truth is out.'

We hadn't been together for long but she had confided in me and this is where it had taken us. Over the next few days the case swung one way and then the other, depending on who was giving evidence. I cannot even begin to imagine how tough it must have been for her to wait for the outcome, but come it did.

'Would the foreman please rise?' asked the clerk of the court in an overly officious voice. 'Do you find the defendant guilty or not guilty?'

I looked up to the gods. 'Please don't let the last few years of struggle be for nothing.'

The verdict came: 'Guilty.'

The wave of relief was overwhelming; my legs were still shaking as the adrenaline slowly started to leave my body.

But let me ask you this: have you ever struggled for something for so long and finally succeeded and reached the summit? Only for you to realize it's not the summit, and that there's a whole new mountain to climb?

That's what happened to us.

Over the next few weeks she became withdrawn and unresponsive. She would sit for hours on end staring up at the ceiling, not talking, just staring into space. She barely ate anything and I was freaking out, not knowing what to do. At this point I was running a successful recruitment company that was doing really well and had generated revenue of £21,000,000. But all the money in the world didn't help, because I didn't know what to do with it!

Out of desperation I checked her into the Priory, a mental health hospital. I was all out of ideas.

I remember looking at the consultant, hoping he had a magic answer. 'Mr Harrington, she is clinically depressed. We are going to give her some tablets to restore her chemical imbalance. She will need to be admitted.'

I think I knew intrinsically that tablets were not the answer – but frankly, at this point, I was willing to try anything.

Fast-forward six weeks and although she has now started speaking again, she was also trashing her room on a regular basis, smoking and in one almighty mess. It was beginning to dawn on me just how lost we both were.

A ray of hope

One night, after visiting her in hospital, I came home and slumped down on the couch. I switched on late-night TV and surfed through the channels, hoping to find something to occupy my mind so I could drift off to sleep.

After a few moments I am glued to the TV screen, I'm feeling a tinge of hope. It was an infomercial by Tony Robbins, the American motivational guru. His message was clear: you can master your own destiny. I hear of his work with celebrities like Andre Agassi, but also ordinary people who have attended his events and had life-changing breakthroughs in their businesses and their private lives. People who had been stuck for years had seemingly magically transformed their circumstances. They seemed like genuine people, too – not weird or funky, but solid, dependable types.

I'm naturally sceptical as I call the freephone number.

'Thank you for calling the Anthony Robbins Companies. Marshonda Henderson here, how may I assist you?'

Marshonda's incredible gift of the gab convinces me to enrol in the Mastery University programme, which is tens of thousands of dollars'-worth of investment.

'What have I got to lose?' I ask myself, and resolve – against all medical advice – to check her out of the Priory Hospital.

A few weeks later, if you had travelled with us, you would have flown to the Orange County Convention Centre in Florida. We had front row seats at Robbins' Unleash the Power Within event. It promised us major breakthroughs, and boy do we need something. I feel like it's my last throw of the dice.

Tony Robbins hits the stage and begins by telling all 5,000 of us that we have the power to change and that later that night we will be walking across hot coals as proof of our power. She is joining in, but I can see she is only going through the motions. I get a sense that her problems are too deeply ingrained for any lasting real change to occur.

'I'm looking for someone who's depressed,' Tony asks the audience. Instinctively, without thinking, I raise her arm. My heart is racing.

One of 'those' moments

As 'luck' would have it, out of those 5,000 people, Tony Robbins chose her to work with one on one. Now picture the scene: the auditorium is huge, with giant screens at the front of the room on either side. There are cameras onstage now, trained on both of us, to capture every nuance of this interaction.

I swallow hard and hope Robbins knows what he's doing.

'So you're depressed? Why are you depressed? Tell me about it,' Robbins commands.

Within a few moments she is tearful, rocking back and forth on her chair in the foetal position, and she's starting to become withdrawn and unresponsive.

'What the hell? How's this going to help?' I'm thinking.

Then he asks her something that totally surprised me. 'Have you ever had an explosive orgasm?'

'Huh?' she asks, incredulously.

'I'm just curious. Have you ever had an explosive orgasm?' he asked again.

'I can't tell you that!' she said coyly. The audience laughs.

'Well you just told 5,000 people about this depressing episode. Why not tell us about this joyful one?'

She's stumped, and looks confused. Robbins calls on help from the audience.

'Ladies and gentleman, can she tell us about this experience – yes or no?'

Five thousand people respond as one with 'Yes!' and clap enthusiastically.

Robbins asks, 'Can you think about that time now? Go back to that time and see what you saw, hear what you heard and feel what you felt.'

She closes her eyes and begins to associate back to the experience. It starts to resemble the scene from the movie *When Harry Met Sally* where Sally (played by Meg Ryan) has a full-blown orgasm in a café.

The crowd cheers her on and it starts to build up – and I mean *really* build up, if you know what I mean. She is flushed in the face and making quite a sound through the microphone she's holding. Now remember, there are cameras onstage looking at us, so the whole audience can see on the big screens what is taking place. You should have seen the look on my face. All I remember thinking was … 'I haven't seen this before!'

This one seminar changed her life. She was totally stuck but came to realize through this intervention that she had the power to choose her emotions depending on what she focused on and the meaning she gave to what happened to her.

I remember thinking, 'I'm so grateful, but what a shame we had to travel internationally to resolve this. And why, when I looked for answers, was I told that tablets were the answer?'

And then, as gentle as a whisper at the back of my mind, I thought, 'Maybe that's why you're here, Andy? Maybe it's meant to be you up there on stage too?'

I was inspired. I wanted to do something similar to Tony Robbins. I wanted to know what he knew and inspire others to make changes in their lives too. But then another thought crept in my mind: 'Don't be ridiculous, Andy. Who's going to listen to you?'

Have YOU ever had a dream, but it just seemed too big? It seems so far away from your starting point that you give up before you've even started?

I told myself to forget about it and stop dreaming. That is, until another Tony Robbins seminar a few months later.

A date with destiny

It's the final day of the Date with Destiny event in Hilton Head Island, South Carolina. We are asked to pair up with a stranger and look directly into their eyes and become really present for them.

This is difficult for me, and I'm a bit slow in finding a partner. It soon becomes apparent everyone has a partner other than me. There are 5,000 people in the room, but I can only see one other person that doesn't have a partner...

Tony Robbins.

Now picture the scene. I'm in Row 16 of around 100 rows of seating. There are security guards all around the stage stopping idiots like me from getting too close to Tony. However, I'm on a mission, and when some guards are distracted I get Tony's attention and motion to him to be my partner. To my complete surprise, he agrees. I proceed to spend five minutes with Tony Robbins that changes the entire direction of my life.

Now I don't know if he remembered I was the partner of the person he had helped, but I looked at him and I was so grateful for what he had done – for all the skill he had, the knowledge he had and the marketing efforts that reached out to me through TV. Tears were pouring from my eyes and to my astonishment I noticed tears rolling down his cheeks, too.

In that moment, I made a life-changing decision. I resolved that even though I was not an expert in any field – not a speaker, an author or a coach – I would learn what I could and seek to help those who like us needed inspiration.

I also secretly dreamt that one day I might share the stage with Tony Robbins.

A passion into profit

It's been almost ten years since the moment I looked into Tony Robbins' eyes and made a life-changing decision to embark on a new career. It's now July 2011.

I'm standing backstage. I can hear the faint murmur of the 9,000 people in the audience as I wait in the holding area of the ExCeL Exhibition Centre in London. I'm not nervous. Having already spoken at the London O_2 Arena to 8,500 people a few months before, I'm more than ready.

I take a moment to reflect over the past decade. My first training company had actually failed, but I'd picked myself up and built a very successful one from the hard-knock lessons I had learned.

I think of my Mum, who looked after me when I felt suicidal after I discovered a long-term partner had cheated on me and left me at my lowest point in my life, both financially and emotionally.

Next to me is Beckie, the single most important person in my life. We had become a couple in the summer of 2009. Her unconditional love for me had given me the courage to start all over again and it had brought me to this point. We are looking forward to our wedding two weeks later.

'This is your moment, Andy, this is all you've dreamt of … I love you baby boy.'

'I love you too Bex.' I pinch myself, because I am about to share the stage with Tony Robbins …!

As I hit the stage I get a standing ovation. I recognize the faces in the audience of those who have been with me on this journey and those who I have helped through my teachings and advice over the last decade. People who I would never have influenced or even met had I not believed in my dream.

Since speaking alongside Tony Robbins in London that day I have spoken in, Ireland, USA, Australia, Singapore, Malaysia, Dubai, South Africa, Poland, Belgium, Holland, Thailand and New Zealand. I've shared the stage with Sir Richard Branson (Virgin), Donald Trump and Alan Sugar (*The Apprentice*), Robert Kiyosaki (*Rich Dad, Poor Dad*), Sir Bob Geldof (Live Aid) Steve Wozniak (Apple co-founder) Jordan Belfort (*The Wolf of Wall Street*), Sebastian Coe (Olympic champion), Brian Tracy, Bob Proctor, Dr John Demartini (*The Secret*), Les Brown, Paul McKenna, Nick Vujicic (the YouTube phenomenon) George Foreman (world heavyweight boxing champion), Erin Brockovich, Larry King, Steve Forbes (*Forbes* magazine), and President of the United States Bill Clinton.

Which brings me right back to November 2012 at the Grosvenor House Hotel in London, where this story started.

The end of a cycle

I can tell from the way he's speaking that Bill Clinton is about to finish his speech. The small, appreciative audience has loved it, but I've been focused on just one man sitting on the top table. At 6 foot 7 inches, Tony Robbins is a towering presence even when sitting down.

By now I have spoken alongside Tony twice, but the truth is, we didn't meet backstage before or after the events – there just isn't time, and Tony generally helicopters in and helicopters out. It's now almost ten years to the day since I committed to become a speaker when I looked into Tony's eyes.

Clinton gets a standing ovation but this is my moment and I make a beeline for Tony Robbins.

I tap him on the shoulder. He turns and stands up.

'Hi Tony, my name's Andy Harrington. I'm not sure if you remember me, but we've shared the stage together alongside Richard Branson and Donald Trump. Could I share a story with you?'

And then it hit me all at once. It feels like déjà vu. I'm almost lost for words. I'm looking once again into those same eyes that I looked into ten years ago.

I update Tony on the last decade and all that has happened and how grateful I am for inspiring me all those years ago. For me, Tony Robbins is the real deal – the original and the best.

Tony Robbins and I at the Bill Clinton Charity Ball following an event at the ExCeL Exhibition Centre in London in 2012.

What I learned is that my life experiences shaped me to be uniquely qualified to do what I do. In life I believe you either win or you learn, and over the years I have learned much and now I give back by teaching others how to turn their passion into profit.

Now it's your turn

In the coming chapters I will reveal how you can go from relative unknown to being a leading light in any subject you choose within just 12–18 months. More importantly, through this book I will prove to you how you can create a real and lasting business turning insane profits so you can create the life you deserve.

Perhaps without being aware of it, you have built up experience, knowledge and knowhow that other people don't yet have. If you have struggled and survived through hard times, you can help someone to do the same. It may have taken you ten years to figure something out – well, now you can help someone to *save* ten years having to figure it all out like you did. If you have come up with a recipe for success, why not package up that knowledge and get paid for sharing it?

YOU a highly paid author, mentor, coach, consultant, speaker or trainer

We are living in the information age. I imagine you have lots of very useful information based on your life experiences to date – some painful, some joyful. Now is the time to capitalize on your hard-earned experience and stop working hard for a living. Instead, start sharing what you know so your wisdom is passed on.

Speaking alongside Tony Robbins and Richard Branson in 2011.

Speaking alongside Donald Trump and Tony Robbins in 2012.

Speaking alongside Richard Branson in South Africa in 2013.

There is an exciting, thriving and lucrative industry awaiting you. Some call it the expert industry, some, the 'how to' or self-help industry. As you enter this industry perhaps you'll deliver your knowledge and knowhow as an author of a 'how to' book, or possibly as an advisor or mentor to high-paying clients; maybe as a coach or consultant; or perhaps even as a highly paid speaker or trainer?

How do you like the sound of travelling the world in business or first class, being treated like a celebrity, and making anything from $20,000 to $500,000 from a single presentation? Sound unlikely? Through this book I will show you how.

Your goal is to motivate people to learn a new skill, brush up on an old one or improve their lives or business in some way. In doing so you'll turn a passion into profit as your reward.

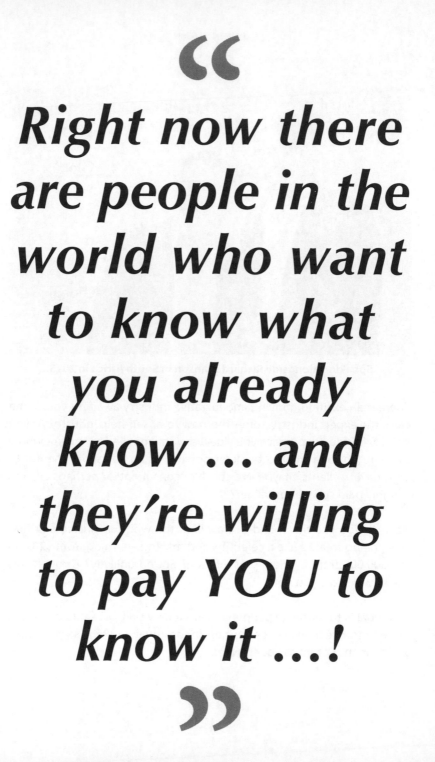

Right now there are people in the world who want to know what you already know ... and they're willing to pay YOU to know it ...!

So let's get started, It promises to be a rollercoaster of a ride, but one I believe you'll love as you come to realize the huge potential to make money, make a difference and leave a lasting legacy.

Speaking to 8,500 people at the London O$_2$ Arena in 2009.

"

'Imagine, if you will, being on your deathbed. And standing around your bed are the ghosts of the ideas, dreams, abilities and talents given to you by life.

'And that you for whatever reason, you never acted on those ideas, you never pursued that dream, you never used those talents, we never saw your leadership, you never used your voice, you never wrote that book.

'And there they are standing around your bed looking at you with large, angry eyes, saying, "We came to you, and only you could have given us life! Now we must die with you forever!"

'The question is – if you die today, what ideas, what dreams, what abilities, what talents and what gifts, would die with you?'

Les Brown

Molly Burr

"

CHAPTER 2

PREPARING FOR A NEW ECONOMY

Allow me to make a bold statement.

You are unique, special and one of a kind. You have been through both good times and bad. As a result, you have learned many important lessons along the way. We don't often think of it, but those life or business lessons have a value.

Through this book I'll show you how to monetize your knowledge and make a small fortune from what you already know, so you can stop working so damn hard every day.

Human beings have evolved enormously since our short time on the planet. How did we do it? The answer: we have shared our knowledge and wisdom.

Thousands of years ago, the elders of tribes would gather their followers round a campfire and tell stories to pass on wisdom based on their life experiences. In doing so the tribe folk would know what to do and what to avoid if they were to encounter a similar situation.

In more recent years, wisdom was passed down through families and through the education system. But here's the problem ...

Families are finding getting around the dinner table together harder to pull off, which means that valuable life lessons are not being passed on. Also, when it comes to life lessons, business, career, or moneymaking knowhow, I think you'll agree, much of what we needed to know we couldn't possibly have learned at school or university.

Right now, ordinary people are on a hunt for answers to personal and professional problems. People are facing situations they are not sure how to deal with and they are willing to pay someone quite a lot of money to avoid pain and move forward.

Why am I telling you this?

Because *you* have many of the answers they are looking for!

We are living in the information age, which means the commodity of the information age is ...? That's right: information. So what do savvy people do to make money in the information age?

The mentoring industry

A whole new 'self-help', 'how to' or 'mentoring' industry has established itself over the last decade. It's not led by celebrities or business tycoons, but by ordinary people like you and I. Real people who have been through real challenges, catastrophes and conflicts, and experienced breakthroughs and changes on a personal and professional level.

Seemingly ordinary people are making it big in the new economy and here's the best part. You need no qualifications other than your life

Thankfully when we lived in tribes, presentation software wasn't invented yet – saving the human race from being wiped out through an epidemic of death by PowerPoint.

experiences, because what makes you as an expert and an authority today is your story of struggle and strive for success, no matter how big or small.

It's not only those who have had problems to overcome that are making it big. It's also people who have followed a passion or pursuit for some time. They have made huge distinctions, which has greatly enhanced their understanding of the subject. Again, these distinctions are valuable, and potentially – with the right marketing – worth millions.

Now at this point, you might be thinking, 'Yes, I have some answers, but I certainly don't have them ALL. So how can I be an authority?'

Good question, but let me ask you this: are you an authority compared to someone who doesn't know what you know? As long as you are a few steps ahead of the people who need your help, you are an authority. Let go of your need to be perfect and to be the finished article, and focus instead on those you can serve with your knowhow.

Business in the information age

Astute business owners have increasingly realized that they need to adapt in order to win more customers too.

People like being sold to only very rarely. The days of cold-calling on our doorsteps is all but over (thankfully), and even cold-calling on the telephone is becoming less and less effective (if it ever was). So guess what clever businesspeople are doing now?

They are sharing knowledge and knowhow for their specific industry. So rather than selling to their potential customers, they are educating them first. Think about it: who are you going to trust? The salesperson who pushes products or services on you and makes you feel uncomfortable, or the expert who teaches you what you need to focus on and what to avoid?

Also, bear in mind the following: *not everyone is ready to buy when you are ready to sell*.

Your potential customers will all be at different points in the buying cycle. But by turning the sales process into an educational one and teaching first, you will move people along the buying cycle more quickly.

Also, those that don't buy from you immediately will almost certainly remember you. If you continue the education process through your marketing efforts, you will stay in the forefront of their mind. So when they are ready to buy, it's YOU they'll come back to, because they know, like and trust you.

Stand out from the crowd

Who are you more likely to want to do business with? The person you have never met before and know nothing about, or the person who wrote a book on the subject, or runs workshops, seminars and webinars, or has audio or video products?

Now you may be thinking, 'Andy, I don't know how to do workshops or products.' Well, the good news is that through this book I am going to show you how to put your ideas and knowhow together, so that others can understand, learn and implement your advice into their lives or business.

In a nutshell, this book will show you how to monetize your knowledge and turn it into a steady stream of income that comes into your bank account even when you sleep!

Don't exchange time for money

Your average person finds a job or starts a small business, and works in that job or business. Unless they go to work, no money is made. The challenge with this approach is that it has no end game. Retirement is the only option if you have a job, which basically means downgrading your life to survive. If you have a small business, your hope is you will sell it one day. But the problem is that *you* are the business, so it's not worth anything without you!

I worked for an insurance company for seven years, working six days a week, often from 8 a.m. until 8 p.m. I answered incoming calls and quoted people for their car insurance. I asked the same questions every day – 'What's your name? What's your date of birth? Where do you live? What car is it?' I think you get the picture. It was very monotonous, and

Molly Burr

what did I have to show for it when I left after seven years of service? A bottle of aftershave … thanks for that!

Create assets and live the life of your dreams

It's not a secret, but rich people don't work for a living; they acquire, create or control assets. Your assets will generate more money than you can ever possibly hope to make exchanging your time for money.

We think of assets as being property, stocks and shares, commodities, currencies, or the physical stock that a business may be holding. However, there is a very lucrative, high-profit asset class that requires no financial outlay and no warehouse to store it.

The most valuable real estate in the world

Your *knowledge* is a tangible asset when it becomes *intellectual property*. This is what lawyers call the value of ideas or information. Intellectual property is the legally recognized, exclusive rights to creations of the mind. In Chapter 6, 'Productizing Your Knowledge', I am going to show you how to take your life experiences and turn them into real value.

Now it is very normal at this point to think, 'Well who am I to proclaim myself a mentor and give advice to people? I'm nobody special.' Consider all the people that also once thought exactly the same thing.

Frank Kern

In 2005, Frank Kern decided to write a book, *Teach Your Parrot to Talk*. This one simple ebook built Frank a $3,000-a-month income stream.

He then said to himself: 'What other pets are out there?'

Frank had worked with dogs in the past, and realized that dogs respond well to positive reinforcement. So he created a course, and created a different website for every different breed of dog. He ran ads for each breed of dog, offering the book across 600 different websites – one per dog breed. This business launched in 2005 and went on to make sales of more than $1 million in 2006.

Frank discovered he enjoyed showing other entrepreneurs how to make money online, so he sold the dog business after two years and focused on teaching people to make money online. Frank now regularly holds live seminars where he commands up to $25,000 per ticket.

Chalene Johnson

Chalene Johnson was working as a paralegal and applied to law school. At the time, personal training was becoming very popular. She began to attend training sessions before and after work, and quickly realized that she had a passion for fitness. Years later, she created a group exercise class that combined dance and kickboxing. This led to the creation of the TurboJam home fitness exercise programme. Since TurboJam, Chalene Johnson has launched TurboKick, PiYo and Hip Hop Hustle, which are available in gyms across the USA and Australia. She has also launched TurboFire, which is a Beachbody DVD exercise programme.

Tony Robbins

My original mentor Tony Robbins began his career promoting seminars for Jim Rohn (another motivational speaker). Later he began his own work as a self-help coach and taught neuro-linguistic programming (NLP) after training with NLP co-founder John Grinder. He later stopped teaching NLP and came up with his own intellectual property instead: the Unleash the Power Within seminars. Tony was a complete unknown when he began. Today his programmes have touched the lives of more than two million people worldwide.

Authority in this industry is gleaned from your life experiences, sometimes from being inspired by someone and often because of a painful situation they had to overcome.

Take the inspirational story of Ruth Driscoll, a very ordinary person who faced enormous personal challenges because of an abusive, controlling relationship.

Now a graduate of my Public Speakers University™ and member of the Professional Speakers Academy™, she teaches other women how to avoid the same trap she was in and how to break free when they are. Her story is truly inspiring and best told by Ruth herself ...

Ruth's story

Lizzie Ayton

Have you ever watched TV when someone else is holding the remote control and they keep pressing the buttons and changing the channel? Well, imagine that remote control is your life and that someone else is pushing the buttons on your life.

It's a pretty horrendous situation for anyone to be in, but for me, a situation I know a great deal about. Let me take you back into my world.

It's a beautiful day. The sun is blazing through the bay window. In the garden beyond I can hear the sounds of birds twittering. Further afield on the cricket pitch I can hear the excited sounds of the players and the thwack of leather on willow. Summer sounds, relaxing sounds, normal sounds. But they couldn't be in greater contrast to the churning of dark emotions I'm feeling inside.

He's entered the room; he's standing there, his shoulders framing the doorway.

Why doesn't he just come right in?

It feels like he's blocking me. I want to rush right past him and escape. I want to march right up to him and yell in his face, 'Get out of my house, and get out of my life.'

But I daren't – I daren't let that emotion show. You learn to do that over the years. You learn to take up a smaller and smaller space inside your own life.

Have you ever found yourself so disgusted with someone you don't even want to look into their face? As I look into his face, which I once considered so handsome, all I see now is the pain and the hurt he has caused. It's like I'm looking into the eyes of some hideous alien being and my lip wants to curl in disgust. But I daren't let it.

I stand frozen, my limbs absolutely still, my face expressionless, my eyes blank. He's standing there in the doorway, his face all sweetness and light. Who would have believed not more than 24 hours ago that face was contorted with rage?

'I'm going to make sure you lose your job. I'm going to make sure your ugly witch face is on every paper in the land. I'm going to make sure you are destroyed!'

And do you know why?

Because I stood up for myself. Because I would not give in to his demands. Because I insisted this time he had to leave my house.

He speaks.

'Darling, I've just got off the phone to the real estate agent, I'm afraid they won't let me sign the contract to go into the flat unless I have someone to act as my guarantor.'

I'm thinking, 'Someone? Someone? He means me. He thinks after all he has done I'm going to sign that paper and become his guarantor!'

But what if I don't sign? He's going to make that the reason why he can't go and I'll never get rid of him. But what if I do sign? He'll never pay his rent or his bills. He will bleed me dry.

But there's something else; there's something more I can feel inside of me. It's like an instinctive behaviour, because I know I'm going to say yes to him. Not because I'm afraid of him, but because whenever someone asks me for help, my automatic reaction is to say, 'Yes, of course I'll help.'

I can feel this happening and I know I've got to suppress it and keep it in. But it's hard. It's like some giant hand is reaching down from the universe and grabbed my guts, and is twisting them into a knot. I don't know how it is I'm still standing. I don't know how the impact of that sensation hasn't doubled me up and sent me tumbling to the floor.

There is a quotation from Buddha that says, 'It does not matter if you win a thousand battles. The greatest conquest is of yourself, for then the victory is truly yours and no-one can take it from you.'

But how do you conquer yourself?

I was the head teacher of a large, challenging inner city school and faced difficulties every day. I was a trained life coach, but I was failing to use my skills to help myself. I knew a great deal about self-development but I wasn't taking any positive action.

I had a decision to make. Should I sign those papers or not? I'm glad to say I didn't. I stood up for myself and told him he had to leave my house regardless.

But I did pay a price. I felt uncomfortable letting go of all I had known. I didn't look after myself and wound up in hospital with the symptoms of a serious medical condition. I was very ill. I had tubes going down my throat and into my stomach. I could barely lift my head off the pillow.

By the time I left hospital I had to relearn how to eat and walk. But most of all I had to relearn how to be Ruth again.

But I still had burning questions inside of me: 'What was that automatic response I had where I was sabotaging myself? What was it about me that made me vulnerable to this man's manipulation and control? What was it about him that made him so pointlessly destructive?'

I had to go on a journey to find out answers to these questions and to find myself again, and on this journey I discovered ...

This is why I'm here. This is my purpose. If that abusive relationship can happen to me, it can happen to anyone.

Now I have coaching programmes and workshops to help people in abusive situations deal with them more effectively, because I know what it feels like and I know what to do about it.

Throughout this book I have included some online re-
sources for you to deepen your understanding. Visit
www.passionintoprofit.info to watch Ruth perform this
story to a live audience. This will demonstrate how she is
able to position herself as an expert for her audience.

So what should you do?

As you can see from Ruth's powerful story, becoming a sought-after
mentor for other people is not about studying in some university lec-
ture theatre and getting letters after your name. Instead your authority
comes from your life experiences and using them to teach others what
to avoid and what to pay attention to, as well as some steps to succeed.

Let's now take a look at the reasons why you might like to join the lucrative mentoring industry and get paid for sharing your advice.

1. You turn your passion into a business

You get to spend time doing what you love. Let's face it, most people
trade time for money so that they can enjoy the little free time they
get. This is no way to live your life. By creating a business around your
passion, everything you do has the resonance of love in it. This has a
compound effect not only to your drive and enthusiasm, but also your
creativity goes through the roof as new levels of energy are released.
Your customers will feel the benefit and so will your bank account.

2. You turn your pain into profit

We have all had painful circumstances in our personal or professional
lives. As a result you have had to figure out how to get out of difficult

situations. You have found ways of coping and I expect you are a better person because of it. You have a unique empathy for people who are facing the same problems, challenges and frustrations that you had.

By creating solutions to these problems, your painful lessons can truly serve you. By teaching others, you transcend way beyond those old problems, cement the changes you have made and reinforce your new-found identity.

Perhaps your pain was a business that had to close? Perhaps you were overweight and now you are slimmer? Maybe you retired and felt lost? Perhaps you lost a loved one and experienced grief? Maybe you felt depressed in the past? Maybe you were stuck in a relationship but now you are free? Potentially in the past you had no clue how to market your business to drive sales, but now you do?

3. You can make money while you sleep

With the advances in technology it is now possible to replicate yourself and make money while you are resting. How is this possible? By pro-ductizing your knowledge and knowhow into books, audios, or videos, which you can sell online while you take a well-deserved rest.

By using online marketing – I'll teach you how in Chapter 7 – you can promote your products and services all around the world.

4. You can help people all over the world

The world is truly your oyster. I regularly have people buy my products while I sleep and awaken to find someone in a far-flung corner of the planet has bought a product of mine online.

Of course it's fantastic to wake up with increased funds in your account. But what is even more stunning is I am now helping someone who lives thousands of miles away and we haven't even met – amazing!

5. Your profit margins are huge

Consider this: what is the cost of six blank CDs? It's most likely around $1 or less. But remember people are not buying blank CDs. They are buying the information on them. In real terms they are buying the transformation and results that your information provides.

What price would you put on a saved marriage, a healthier life, increased sales or productivity, investment advice, marketing knowhow, or overcoming challenging personal trauma?

If you sold your six-CD set for $297, deduct $1 for the CDs and let's say $10 for the cases, you are making a whopping $286 in profit. That's a profit margin of 96 per cent. You work once to produce the asset (in this case, the audios) and you get paid forever.

Of course you could make even more profit by offering the product as a digital download and then you have no costs at all!

6. You can travel all over the world

Once you have been selling your products all over the world, you could also choose to put on a workshop to deepen the learning experience of all the people who bought your audio programme.

This means you get to travel the world and make money rather than spend it. Wow – what a concept! I have conducted seminars in Sydney, Melbourne, Brisbane, Adelaide, Perth, Singapore, Kuala Lumpur,

Johannesburg, Cape Town, Dubai, Warsaw, Amsterdam, Brussels, Antwerp, Dublin, London, USA and Canada all in the last 12 months.

7. You work more effectively one-to-many, NOT just one-to-one

In order to make the kind of life-changing income most people dream of, you have to help a lot of people. You can make money by serving others with a product or service. The beauty of the 'how to' or mentoring industry is that you get to help lots of people all at once. Here's how I do it:

- Do group mentoring days of up to 150 people at a time.

- Do webinars of up to 1,000 people at a time.

- Speak on stage to audiences of up to 9,000 people.

- Record videos, which are sent to hundreds of thousands of people online.

It just makes obvious sense when I am working one-to-many that I am making the best use of my time, helping more people and therefore making more money!

In a nutshell

- *Your knowledge is valuable to others who don't know what you know.*

- *You don't need qualifications. Your experiences give you authority.*

- *You don't need to be a celebrity to start, but you might become one.*

- *Your knowledge can be monetized.*

CHAPTER 3

POSITIONING YOURSELF AS AN 'EXPERT' AUTHORITY

If I say to you 'running shoe', which company do you automatically think of? Chances are, you thought of Nike. There are many companies that make and market running shoes, but most likely you thought of just one. Now why is that?

Because Nike effectively owns a piece of your brain. To be precise, it owns a neural circuit that fires off when you think about running shoes, and you'll pay a premium to buy their products because of their 'expert' status.

Positioning establishes what a person or their company is known for. It establishes their brand identity. It clarifies their values, beliefs and, most importantly, what they stand for. All of this serves to both attract the right type of customers to your advice-sharing business and repel the wrong kind of people too.

The benefits of being seen as an expert are considerable. Too many brilliant mentors, coaches, consultants, authors, trainers, speakers and seminar leaders are not being paid what they are worth because they haven't positioned themselves in the minds of their audience.

Consider the difference between a health practitioner and Jason Vale, who is known worldwide as 'the Juice Master'.

Jason's story

Jason's story is incredible.

There was a point in Jason's life where he hit rock bottom. He was suffering from severe psoriasis, eczema, asthma, hay fever and obesity. He was smoking two to three packets of cigarettes a day and drank very heavily – up to 14 pints of beer a day.

He discovered that juicing vegetables and a little fruit as his main tool to clear his skin. He lost weight and freed himself of illness. Now Jason is on a mission to 'juice the world' and help people to turn their health around using natural means.

He put a stake in the ground and announced himself as the Juice Master. He mentored people, put on seminars and workshops, and then wrote a bestselling book entitled Slim for Life.

In 2002 Jason was asked by Moulinex to be the face of its juicers. Moulinex soon became the bestselling juicer in the country. In 2005, Philips headhunted Jason to be the face of its range of juicers and blenders in the UK and throughout Europe. Philips' product soon became, and remained, the bestselling juicer during Jason's endorsement.

In 2013, Tristar Products approached Jason to be the new 'Jack La Lanne' in the USA. Jason became a real hit in the US, so Tristar extended the agreement to make it global: Jason is now the worldwide face of the Fusion range of juicers and blenders.

Jason regularly appears on radio and television, and in the press. He also put together the ground-breaking film, Super Juice Me! One Disease – One Solution? The UK premiere took place in London's West End, at the prestigious Odeon cinema on Leicester Square to a celebrity-packed audience. The film has received five-star reviews and hundreds of thousands of people went to see it in its first week.

Jason has worked with big name celebrities such as Jennifer Aniston, Drew Barrymore, Sarah Jessica Parker, Gary Lineker, Naomi Campbell, Katie Price and Alesha Dixson.

Jason also runs retreats in beautiful facilities in Portugal and Turkey that are sold out months and month in advance.

Why did all this happen? Well, for one, Jason is now a very talented speaker, coach, mentor, marketer and business owner, but it all started because he made the decision to position himself as the Juice Master.

You can find out more about Jason and his incredible journey at his website, www.juicemaster.com.

Be a specialist

I strongly suggest you avoid being a generalist as this is an overcrowded market with lots of providers charging fees that are far too low. Take a step up and be a specialist so that eventually you become known as an expert. Over time, if you follow the advice in this book, you'll become an authority as you publish and promote your ideas through workshops, webinars, seminars, audio programmes, videos on YouTube and your own website, and through a book that I will help you to write.

There is also the possibility you will achieve the highest status for the mentoring industry, which is to be known as a celebrity expert like a Jason Vale, or a Tony Robbins, or a Robert Kiyosaki, author of *Rich Dad, Poor Dad*.

Your very first step in turning your passion into profit is to put a stake in the ground and claim your subject – the topic on which you will come to be known for and identified by others as a leading expert. It is important in the beginning that you choose just one subject to become known for as you establish yourself.

I am known as an expert authority in public speaking, motivation, mindset and marketing, but in the beginning it was just mindset. Over time you may become known as an expert in other subjects too, but begin with only one. Trying to be a 'Jack of all trades' will leave you being master of none. Make no mistake; you will need to master your subject if you are going to make it to the top.

Here's a quick guide to help you choose your initial subject ...

1. Passion

Choose a subject on which you have a deep passion. You'll know you are passionate about a subject if you devote your most precious resource to it. Time.

What do you love to spend time doing, learning, watching or studying? What would you do even if you weren't going to get paid for doing it? What is a hobby or an avid interest that you have been following for some time that has caused you to make some distinctions others would not have made? What is a subject you have invested your own hard-earned money on to experience, or to evolve your ability?

2. Pain

Is there a subject that became a primary focus for you because of a big problem? Perhaps you experienced a personal loss or pain in your life or business, which sent you on a quest, a voyage of personal discovery, a hunt for a solution?

Potentially you feel this is your calling – that you have been shaped to become the person you are today because of this pain, and now you feel it's time to give back to those who are going through what you endured?

3. Practice

Select a topic you are willing to practice day and night to perfect, making finer and finer distinctions. Choose a subject that would not feel like work to you to make those distinctions but instead would feel like play. Top sportspeople put in what would seem to others like painstaking hours of practicing, but these people live in the 'forward'. They project themselves into the future and see the very moment when the practice will pay off for the biggest reward. When the clock is counting down and it's going down to the wire for them, that's the time they planned for, and they seize the moment and create history.

4. Performance

Is there a subject on which you have high levels of natural ability? For others it may seem difficult or even impossible, but for you it's easy to perform better than others? You may not even know at this point why or how you find it easy, but you just do. Other people will probably have voiced how gifted you seem or maybe they even called you lucky.

5. Personality

It is very important to choose a subject that fits your personality type. Without doubt, the best profiling tool I have come across is Talent Dynamics. I thoroughly recommend doing this not just for you, but also for the people you will employ as part of your team. Making sure you select the right people for the right job is crucial in building a world-class team and building a successful 'expert' business.

6. Profitable

Finally, once you think you have found your subject, the last sanity check is to establish if there are good profits to be made from the subject. You'll need to be sure that there are people who are hunting for information to master the subject themselves or to solve a problem that they have. Remember, all businesses must sell a product or service to make profit, and all products or services must solve a problem or enhance people's lives to be of value. Also, consider the longevity of the subject. Will it be a passing fad or an evergreen topic that people will always want solutions for?

Below are some evergreen profitable subjects:

- Leadership

- Investing

- Productivity

- Sales

- Motivation

- Spirituality

- Marketing

- Health

- Parenting

- Business

- Relationships

- Communication.

Align with your audience

If you are like most people starting out, you will believe that your message is for everyone. You have a burning ambition to help as many people as possible and you want to spread your message far and wide. However, this is a huge mistake. Even if it's true that your subject is for all, it's impossible to market to everyone because of the cost!

Trust me on this one. When I started out, I tried a quarter-page advert in a national newspaper with a readership of well over one million people. Guess how many people responded to the ad? That's right – zero …!

So what to do instead?

You are much better off defining your audience in a more narrow way so that it's easier to reach them with a targeted marketing message that directly appeals to them and their hopes, dreams and desires.

When you are able to define your potential audience better, you'll be able to find places to get in front of them through various media at a much reduced price.

For example, my subject area is communication skills; but more specifically, my target audience is entrepreneurial people who want to put a message together and make millions from sharing it. My target audience are people like you who want to improve the quality of their lives by improving the quality of their audience's lives. My target audience is entrepreneurs who may want to use public speaking as a way of selling more products and services.

In my niche there are many people who help people overcome, say, the fear of public speaking. But I don't specialize in that. Now don't get me wrong – I can help you become a world-class speaker, even if you are nervous. But it's not the market I'm going after. Does that make sense?

Who do you have empathy for?

Choosing an audience also means considering the kind of people you want to spend time with. If you are going to be a huge success, you are going to be communicating regularly with your audience through emails, videos, Facebook posts, tweets, blogs, face-to-face and (potentially) live onstage performances. So guess what? You had better like the people you serve, because you're going to be spending time communicating and interacting with them.

Perhaps there are a group of people you have a unique empathy for? A special understanding of the kinds of problems, challenges and frustrations they face? Maybe you went through similar situations to the ones they face?

Personally, I love working with entrepreneurial people – people who think positive and want to build something that may even outlast themselves. I like possibility people who are prepared to take risks in the pursuit of their dreams. I like people who refuse to settle for something less than they are capable of. I like outspoken people who are prepared to speak the truth rather than just be nice. I like people who hold themselves and others to a high standard.

Sound like you? I hope so, because even though I don't know you yet, I hope to. I believe there is much we can do together to make a sizable shift in the quality of life for the people we choose to serve.

Know your audience

There is an old truism: 'Know your audience'. But what does it really mean to know your audience? What specifically do we want to know and why?

Knowing your audience affords us the ability to position ourselves in their minds as their 'go to' expert when they have a problem they need to solve. Remember, not everyone is ready to commit to a financial transaction the very first time they get to know about you. But at some point they will hit a pain threshold, when the desire for a solution becomes urgent and immediate. That is when they need to think of you and know where to find you.

At the very moment they go on a hunt for a solution. You must be positioned as their number one choice. At this point your marketing and positioning should have created a feeling of knowing, liking and trusting you as a source of hope and help.

Without realizing it, your positioning has been creating a belief in the mind of your audience about you. Your marketing (more about this in a later chapter) has been fostering a relationship of trust with your audience. Now, because they need you, that trust is about to be tested by a financial transaction in their hour of need.

However, without first getting to know your audience you will never create a bond or connection that encourages them to open up to you.

Problems = opportunity

In simple terms there are just two things you need to know about your audience, although later you can delve deeper and discover more:

- What problems does your audience need to solve specifically?

- What results does your audience want to achieve?

Here are some questions for you to discover exactly what you need to know about *your* audience. To discover their problems, ask:

- My ideal customer is not good at …

- My ideal customer is uncertain of …

- My ideal customer no longer wants to experience …

- My ideal customer doesn't want to feel …

- My ideal customer believes …

- My ideal customer has nightmares about …

To discover what results your audience wants to achieve, ask:

- My ideal customer needs to become better at …

- My ideal customer wants to be certain of …

- My ideal customer wants to experience …

- My ideal customer wants to feel …

- My ideal customer needs to believe …

- My ideal customer dreams of …

The answers to these questions are golden nuggets of information that will help you to formulate everything you'll create to reach and teach this audience. You'll have the base material for your start, your story, your solution and your sale.

Why should I listen …?

Today I am fortunate to be invited to speak all around the world in giant seminars of 5,000 to 10,000 people at a time. I am honoured to have spoken on stage alongside the true leaders and the movers and shakers of the world. So when a crowd flocks to hear Richard Branson, Tony Robbins, Donald Trump or Bill Clinton speak, they are not necessarily coming to hear Andy Harrington speak, as I am not as well-known as these titans of wealth and business. Well, not yet, anyway.

However, by the end of my presentation, they have grown to know, like and trust me to the point they have immediately invested several thousands of their hard earned money to enrol in my advanced courses.

So when I begin my presentation, I must use all my skills to answer four vital questions in the minds of the audience.

1. Why should I listen?

To answer this question I must create content in the first few moments of my presentation that speaks directly to the hopes, dreams and aspirations of the audience. I must then move to highlighting the problems, challenges and frustrations they face in trying to achieve this. In doing so, I *position the audience* so they are *my audience*.

2. Why should I listen to **this**?

To answer this question, I must create content that positions why focusing on and mastering my subject area will help my audience to accelerate their ability to overcome the obstacles to achieving their goals. I must build the case for why this is true and, in doing so, *position my subject* as the solution to their current challenges

3. Why should I listen to this **now**?

Let's face it – we live in busy times. There is so much competing for our attention. So if your audience can put off doing something, the chances are they probably will. So here I have to create content that increases motivation to focus their attention *now*. I must show them the consequences of inaction and the cost of not solving their current problems, and then I must show them where the opportunity is right now, based on both where they and the world are at right now.

4. Why should I listen to **you**?

Audiences are naturally sceptical. We tend to guard the gates to our minds against what and who we allow to influence us. Until this question is answered, your audience remain closed – and although they may appear to be listening to you, they are not going to change or behave differently as a result. I begin to open them up to being influenced by me through *positioning myself* as the 'go to' expert authority, and the best way to facilitate this is through the telling of a personal story.

The strategy I have just outlined will work perfectly if you are producing an online video for your website. It will be spot on if you are speaking to a corporation as an outside consultant or trainer. It will open people up if you are an employee needing to get a message across in a meeting to your fellow employees.

It will do wonders for you if you are working with the general public. It will work as the beginning of your book. Finally, it will help you nail it whether your audience is five or 5000 people.

> *Throughout this book I have included some online resources for you to deepen your understanding. This chapter's resource is to visit **www.passionintoprofit.info** and watch a video recording of a live performance of the first few minutes of one of my presentations as I position the audience, my subject and myself as an expert. You'll find it under the heading 'Chapter 2: Positioning yourself as the "go to" expert'.*

In a nutshell

- *Decide who you will serve.*

- *Emphasize what makes you unique.*

- *Put a stake in the ground and claim your subject.*

- *Position yourself as the 'go to' guru for your audience.*

"

If you don't want to preach ... ... put a story in your speech!

"

CHAPTER 4

PROVING CREDIBILITY WITH A PERSONAL STORY

O f all the mediums of persuasion, a story is the most eloquent and subtle. You'll need to persuade people that you are someone they can trust as a source of hope, help and information to solve a situation that they are facing in their personal or business lives.

As humans, we have been listening to stories since the dawn of communication. When it comes to positioning yourself as the 'go to' guru for your industry, you must design, develop and deliver a personal story.

No one likes being told what to do, or being lectured. In the beginning your audience are naturally sceptical and still guarding the doors of their mind to see if they can trust you before allowing themselves to be influenced. The beauty of a story is that it captivates the mind and allows for influence to occur unconsciously and indirectly.

Your story should do two things:

1 Position you as an expert

Your story absolutely must prove why you have become knowledgeable in your subject. But – crucially – remember that you need to demonstrate your knowhow comes not just because of some certificate or qualification, but also or instead because of your experiences. Your story must reveal how you have come to know what you now know about your subject. Typically, your knowledge will have been motivated by either inspiration or desperation (or maybe both). Your job when designing your story is to look at your life experiences and pull from them that initial spark of desire to overcome or achieve, followed by your journey to get to where you are today,

2 Provide a valuable lesson along the way

A common mistake I see here from mentors, authors, coaches, consultants and speakers is to tell a story that sounds like a CV. A chronological series of events is *not* a story – it's just plain boring. Plus, a story is for an audience. Yes, it must position you as an authority, but if that's all it does, you are going to come across like some conceited, self-absorbed narcissist. This means that the focus of your story should be the audience and therefore it must be a story that also provides a valuable lesson. Just remember that the goal here is to allow the audience to extract the message from the story themselves rather than have you tell them 'The moral of the story is ...'

Vulnerability is a strength

For many people, the idea of telling a personal story can be somewhat daunting. However, if you want to build rapport and a genuine feeling of trust with your audience, a story is the way to go. Does this mean you may have to become vulnerable when you tell your story? Yes; but I'm not talking about the kind of vulnerability that comes from being broken or open to being hurt. I'm talking about the kind of vulnerability that comes from being honest, genuine and real.

By opening yourself up and telling a real story, where you disclose to the audience a struggle you went through, or a conflict you were wrestling with, you begin to engender trust. We only normally reveal ourselves to people we know well like our family and closest friends. So when we tell a personal story, in effect we trust the audience with this information. We are laying down the foundations of friendship. Now here's what's interesting: trust is a two-way street. By being trusting, we are also seen as trustworthy.

But I don't have a story

At this point you may be thinking, 'But Andy, I don't have a story. What would I say in my story? Who would be interested anyway?' It is natural for you to have these thoughts, but over the rest of this chapter I will reveal to you how there is an amazing story based on your life experiences that will help position you as an authority.

Today, the very best storytellers are found in Hollywood. A movie can keep us gripped for a few hours and on the edge of our seats, totally engaged. So how do they do that? And more importantly, how can you get the same results in the story that positions you as the 'go to' expert for your industry?

What follows is a system for telling a personal story. When you use it, it will transform your standing in your industry and compel your audience to see you as a trusted source of information and the solution to their challenges.

Curiosity killed the cat

Think of one of your favourite movies. I am willing to bet that when you first began to watch it, you weren't entirely sure what was happening, who was who and how they related to each other, what their history was and how they were going to react to situations.

Whenever we watch a great movie for the first time, I guarantee that you the viewer will have unanswered questions. A well put together story should raise questions in the minds of the audience and then answer these questions while raising new ones.

What does this all mean to you? Don't make your story predictable!

Questions equal interest

Have you ever watched a really poor movie that you carried on watching it to discover just how poor it really was? Why did you do it? Probably because there were unanswered questions in the film that made you watch it all the way through to get those answers, only to ask when they came, 'Is that *it* …?'

Too many speakers insult their audience's intelligence by over explaining the story rather than hinting or allowing the characters interactions with each other tell the story.

Go back right now and re-read the prologue and Chapter 1 of this book. You will discover line by line I am raising unanswered questions in your mind as the story unfolds. This serves to keep you interested because there is a part of your brain that can't cope with incompleteness, and so you keep on reading to find out what happens. In doing this you as the reader (or listener) are doing some of the brainwork.

Narration v. dialogue

A story can be told through narration, or it can be relived through the dialogue between the characters. Hollywood very rarely tells a story using narration. We only ever find out what is taking place through what the characters say to each other and what we see on the screen.

Imagine watching your favourite movie and instead of hearing the dialogue between the characters, they dub on a voiceover, which tells you what is going on! Do you think that might spoil your enjoyment of it somewhat?

The truth is, the movie would most likely become boring pretty quickly. And the reason for that is because narration is always describing something AFTER it has already happened which means we as the viewer will feel dissociated from the story.

Hearing the responses from the characters in real time not only tells us the information we need to know in the story, it also introduces emotion. We can hear from their words how they are feeling. This appeals to the right hemisphere of our brains as we begin to understand the motives of each character. This in turn often takes us on a voyage of self-discovery as we identify a part of ourselves as being like them.

In addition, Hollywood also knows a very powerful trick it must pull off if it is going to grab and keep our attention.

Put the audience in the scene

Hollywood wants and needs you to care about the main character. In a romantic comedy, you need to care whether the lead couple gets together or not. In a thriller, you need to care if the hero will get there in time to save the day. A captivating 'whodunit' will encourage you to try to figure out who is responsible, and an effective horror movie will make you care about who lives or dies. Hollywood wants you to feel the tension and the uncertainty of the main characters 'as if you were there, in real time'. It achieves this they with great camera work so that, at key moments, it feels as if you are having the same dilemma and drama as the central characters.

When we feel as if we are really there, something truly remarkable takes place, which is often the main reason for the story. I'll explain with an example.

Have you seen the movie *Titanic*? In the film there is a scene where some of the passengers manage to get onto one of the lifeboats and row a safe distance from the sinking ship.

Initially we see an establishing shot where we, the viewer, see the lifeboat from a side view (as if we were in another lifeboat). However, the very next camera angle has us looking over a passenger's shoulder as if we were in the main lifeboat, where a debate is taking place. Do you remember the debate?

There is screaming all around the boat and cries for help as other passengers of the Titanic are struggling in the icy waters of the North Atlantic Ocean. The debate is whether they should turn back and save people or remain safe in their lifeboat.

Because of the camera work that placed you in the boat, you can't help but to think as you watch the scene unfold, 'Now, what would I do?'

Great stories have a habit of getting us emotionally connected with the main characters. When there is a dilemma, we feel their pain. In doing so, we get to evaluate what is important to us and it can strengthen or even change what we believe to be morally right, it can shift our perspective.

S.A.V.E. the scene

However amazing your story is, as far as the brains of your audience members are concerned, it is simply information. I tell you this because understanding how the mind receives and processes information is crucial to the design of your personal story.

Our mind needs a container to hold the data of the story, otherwise the story is too loose and difficult to follow. When it comes to a story, well-crafted scenes help the audience to know where they are in time and space.

At my Public Speakers University (www.publicspeakersuniversity.com), the mistake I see most often when a student is telling their story happens when they describe the actions of the characters in the story but without first building the scene. The mistake the speaker makes is to forget that the audience cannot see what is in the speaker's head unless they describe it …!

If you were to tell a story about an event that had happened in your life, you would be recalling the images of it, including some peripheral details about the scene. This helps you to see what takes place within the scene.

Building the scene for the audience allows them to be there with you. I have my students S.A.V.E. the scene.

- **Smells:** Is there anything you can refer to engage the sense of smell?

- **Auditory:** Are there any sounds you can mention?

- **Visual:** Paint a picture of the scene, so that your audience can see where they are.

- **Emotions:** Does the scene have a feeling to it?

I'm not suggesting you need to spend long building the scene and you don't need to use the entire S.A.V.E. formula each time. Let's take a quick review of part of Ruth Driscoll's story as she builds the scene for the audience in the beginning.

> *'It's a beautiful day. The sun is blazing through the bay window. In the garden beyond I can hear the sounds of birds twittering. Further afield on the cricket pitch I can hear the excited sounds of the players and the thwack of leather on willow. Summer sounds, relaxing sounds, normal sounds. But they couldn't be in greater contrast to the churning of dark emotions I'm feeling inside.'*

Having now set the scene, Ruth can go on to describe the actions, thoughts, conversations and conflict that ensue. Notice also how she speaks in the present tense, allowing you to experience the scene as if it were happening right now. This serves to bring you right into the scene as if you were right there with her.

A story must not be told, it must be relived

I have already stressed the importance of dialogue v. narration in the story. Dialogue implies there will be conversations taking place between the characters, which in turn means there has to be some other characters other than YOU in the story.

There a three ways your audience can relate to the characters in the story.

1. They must be able to SEE them

It seems obvious, but so many storytellers don't take the time to describe the characters in the story. When this happens, the audience are a little lost, as they can't picture this person. The description does not have to be lengthy and could be more of a hint of what this character looks like. It should also not be a detour from the story but flow naturally. Let's review briefly again a part of my expert-positioning story as I describe one of the characters.

'In the dock is a small, boyish-looking girl in her early 20s with short, dark hair giving evidence. Her chin is on her chest. She's just been cross-examined and it's not gone well. After a few moments that seem like eternity, her own counsel asks her one final question.'

It is also useful sometimes to give a character a trait name that refers to their characteristics. This too can serve to help the audience see them better.

'As I open the old wooden oak door, a man with a towering, domi-nating presence confronts me. His briefcase has seen better days. He pushes his spectacles onto his nose. He's everything you'd imagine Mr Officious to be ...'

Because we have now created a trait name for this character, all I have to do in the story if I want to refer to him is say 'Mr Officious', and the audience will recall the image I just painted in their minds.

2. Characters can be SHAPED for the audience

Shaping your characters means giving depth to their character – per-haps hinting at the kind of person they really are, their values, beliefs, and principles. It may even be useful to mention some historical data about this person so that the audience is able to make a value judgment about them. Essentially, the audience needs to begin to put them into the category of a goodie or a baddie ...!

Let's add some depth to Mr Officious to show you how this is done.

'As I open the old wooden oak door, a man with a towering, dominat-ing presence confronts me. **His eyes seem to pierce right through me. Perhaps that's because he's spent the previous three years**

in jail for a crime he says he didn't commit. *His briefcase has seen better days. He pushes his spectacles onto his nose. He's everything you'd imagine Mr Officious to be ...'*

3. Characters' CONVERSATIONS tell the story

The trap most storytellers fall into is to tell the story through narration. There is a place for narration, as too much dialogue can make it sound like a stage play. However, the key turning points should always be told through either dialogue between the characters or through inner dialogue as we the audience get to hear what they are saying to themselves, or what they are thinking.

No struggle, no story

Your story should be about transformation. No story is worth telling unless change occurs in the hero or in us the audience. The bigger the growth, the more epic the tale.

For growth and transformation to occur at some point in the story the main protagonist (you) has to experience a setback or problem from which you will ultimately attempt to overcome.

Your story should depict you initially as a slightly flawed character (which you will later transcend), but a character your audience will soon empathize with and come to like and care for, as they see at heart you are a good person.

Soon in the story you are facing a challenge represented by a conflict between you and the main villain. This sees you catapulted on a journey where you hope to win the battle and, in doing so, you'll grow in character in the eyes of the audience.

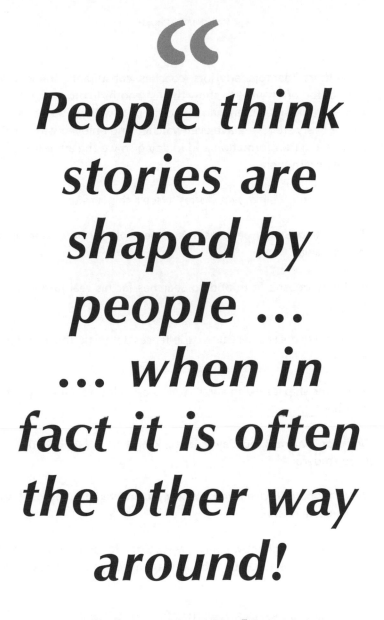

People think stories are shaped by people ...

... when in fact it is often the other way around!

Terry Pratchett

Expert authors, mentors, advisors, coaches, consultants, trainers, and speakers all too often want to show their strengths in order to influence people. But remember: there can be no strength without a weakness to overcome. Every story we have ever watched and enjoyed was because we witnessed a transformation and in doing so we the audience go on that journey with them.

Let's look at some well-known stories to see if this is true:

- *The Lion King*: Simba believes he's responsible for his father's death and runs away.

- *Elf*: Buddy doesn't fit in and so searches for his real father for the answers.

- *Sleeping with the Enemy*: Laura experiences domestic abuse and must escape.

- *Titanic*: The ship is sinking and so is Rose's loveless relationship, which traps her.

- *Gladiator*: Maximus must avenge the killing of his family and his beloved emperor.

- *The Shawshank Redemption*: Wrongly convicted for murder, Andy must survive prison.

Stop and consider right now your answers to the following questions, for within those answers may be the foundations for your expert positioning story.

- What adversities have you faced?

- What has shaped you to be the person you are today?

- Why do you have such strong beliefs about certain things?

- What's the journey you've been on?

- Who have you been battling with?

- What have you had to endure?

- What do you stand for, and why?

- What loss did you have to deal with?

- What failure did you have to come back from?

- Who rejected or marginalized you?

- What's a situation that called for you to muster all your courage?

- How did you get to where you are today?

Outward struggle, inner conflict

I have been teaching positioning through storytelling long enough to know that you will need an adversary for your story, so the main character has a competitor to battle against.

Your adversary could be a person or it could be a group of people. It may not even be a person; it could be a corporation. In Ruth's story earlier in this book the opponent was her partner, who was controlling and abusing her. In my story, in scene one it was the defendant at the back of the court. In scene two it was the doctor who prescribed the drugs and in the next scene initially it was Tony Robbins, who appeared to be making the problem worse, although he didn't.

The peculiar thing about an outward struggle is that it nearly always becomes an internal one. In your story, show how you faced a dilemma, made a difficult decision, and ultimately broke through and transformed beyond your circumstances.

In Ruth's story, she had to suppress her instinctive urge to say yes to people and allow herself to be controlled and manipulated.

In *The Lion King*, Simba must face the dilemma of doing the right thing, returning to the Pride Lands and facing his past or staying in the wilderness and living 'Hakuna Matata'.

If you want to have more impact, you'll also want to build the conflict so that it increases in intensity. You don't want to introduce the conflict only for it to be solved and all over in the next sentence. *Titanic* would not have been the epic it became if the ship had hit the iceberg and then sank two minutes later ...!

When you build the tension in your audience, they become more and more involved in your story. They become fascinated as they witness the attempts that you make to solve the problem and the contrasting reactions of the characters.

If you remember in *Titanic*, as the ship begins to sink some people continue to eat their dinner. Some passengers believe the Titanic is an unsinkable ship, while others start to panic. The rich people try to pay their way onto the lifeboats, only to be told, 'I'm sorry, your money has no currency here!' One member of the crew shoots himself, as he can't cope with the responsibility of deciding who gets on the lifeboats and lives and who stays on the Titanic and faces a probable death. While all this is taking place, the musicians continue to play, doing what they love in the final moments.

As you think about your own personal struggle, consider how it built. What did you try initially that didn't work? What strategies did you employ? What avenues did you go down, only to realize it was a dead end? What did you do that seemed to be the answer, only to discover it wasn't and you were back to square one again?

The summit scene

The conflict and struggle within your own personal story must build to a crescendo, climb to a climax or reach a summit. You must create a moment in time where something has to give. Your story has reached its pivotal moment. At the summit of your story there has to be a new insight, a discovery or a revelation. Something happens that changes everything – you then make a breakthrough and it is often followed by a new commitment.

Too many expert positioning stories are ruined by a non-existent or poorly performed summit scene. You must take the audience to the very moment you made your breakthrough so that they make the breakthrough with you. This is where you reveal the source of the inspiration that took you to where you are today and why you are perfectly positioned to be a source of hope and help to them.

In *The Lion King*, the summit scene occurs when Simba is faced with the task of going back to the Pride Lands and doing the right thing, but also having to risk facing his past. He is lost and longs for his father. At this point, wise old Rafiki guides him to the water's edge and tells him to take a look.

'That's not my father, it's just my reflection,' he laments.

'No … look harder,' Rafiki encourages.

The waters change and we see a reflection in the water of Simba's father Mufasa.

'You see? He lives in you.'

The clouds above Simba part and we hear Mufasa telling Simba: 'Remember who you are. You are my son and the one true king. Remember, remember.'

Before and after

What makes a great story so influential is often the difference between where our character starts in the story and who they ultimately become by the end. Contrast seems to have a huge effect on us humans, as it gives us two points on which to measure a change. The easiest way to sell a weight loss product is to have a picture of an overweight person before using the product and a second picture of the same person having now lost the weight.

Knowing this, you must paint for your audience the 'before picture' early in the story to set up the contrast with your 'after picture', which will come later. Your 'after picture' is where you will position yourself as an expert authority based on your achievements, the work you do today and the people you serve. The key here is to remember that your ultimate positioning will be greatly magnified by your story of struggle to get there.

In one of my personal stories, I describe the contrast of how in my first ever presentation in front of a live audience of just five people I was so nervous I was fiddling with the flipchart pen by constantly removing and replacing the lid as I spoke. Not only was this terribly annoying and distracting for the audience, I was horrified to discover when I had finished and went to restroom that I had been performing for several minutes with black ink all over my forehead!

When I share that today I have spoken in giant arenas all over the world with audiences of 9,000 people, it shows a contrasting 'before and after'

Molly Burr

My first public performance was not the best.

that serves to convince the audience they too can succeed—even if they are just a beginner.

Zero to hero

One of my greatest professional joys is taking someone new to the mentoring industry and helping them to build their personal story and position themselves as the 'go to' person for their industry.

I love giving people the opportunity of speaking alongside me on a big stage somewhere in the world. For me, it's always fascinating to see a speaker who has been trained to a high standard; if you add a *big* audience, you often witness a peak in their performance. Consider the story of Vivian Wijaya from Indonesia.

Vivian had recently attended the Public Speakers University and gone on to become one of the Elite members of the Professional Speakers Academy. Elite Members receive exclusive seven-day training with me plus ongoing mentoring from my Academy Coaching Executive (ACE) team.

Vivian was sitting in one of my training sessions when I unexpectedly announced that she was to speak alongside Nick Vujicic (the YouTube phenomenon), Les Brown, Brendan Burchard and myself in Singapore to an audience of 5,000 people.

A few days later, when I saw her initial video of her story, I thought we had bitten off more than we could chew to get her ready in time. Vivian was making all the classic mistakes, and the story was flat and boring. However, her ACE Team Mentor Cheryl Chapman used the principles I have outlined here; when Vivian told her story, she had the audience gripped and on the edge of its seats. In doing so, she perfectly positioned herself as an expert.

See how many of the techniques you can spot discussed in this chapter in the story of Vivian Wijaya. It is shown here in Vivian's voice.

Vivian's story

Have you ever had a dream?

In 2005, if you had been with me you would have seen me achieve a dream. I'm wearing a white coat, and I have a degree on my shoulder that says MB, BCH and BAO. I'm a medical doctor.

I have a wardrobe full of designer clothes and a sports car in my garage and I'm earning a pretty good living for someone my age. I'm living a dream.

But it's someone else's dream.

What about my dream? Does it matter? And, what was my dream?

Let's go back to 1984 and find out what happened.

'Mummy, I just made my first ever comic book. Would you have a look and tell me what you think?'

'Wow, darling, let me see. This is amazing – you created all this and you're only six! I'm impressed. I think one day you are going to be world-famous and this book is going to sell millions.'

My mother was very supportive of my dream initially, but things changed as I grew up. One day my mother, who looks like an older version of me, with her brown eyes, gave me this look, which I had never seen, in her face before. She said:

'My daughter, I understand how important it is, this whole comic book thing. You've been doing it for years. You show it to your friends, they all cheer and it makes you feel good. But you have to understand that this is just a hobby. It's not going to be a career. It's not going to earn you a living. You're 14. You have to start thinking about your future and what you want to do with the rest of your life.

'But you're lucky, because your father and I have thought of a very good career path for you. You can be a medical doctor. We're going to pay for the education. All you have to do is ace the grades and get into medical school. Can you do that for me?'

'Mum, no offence, and don't get me wrong – I have nothing against being a medical doctor. Dad is one and he is well respected by every-one because of that, I really appreciate that. But what I really want to

do with my life is become a successful comic book creator, a cartoonist like Walt Disney. You know that because I've been saying that since I was aged two. What's with all this fuss?'

'Vivian, I am sick and tired of this conversation. For so many years you never ever listened to a word I said. This time, if you don't get into med school, then you aren't my daughter anymore, do you understand? End of discussion.'

Have you ever had someone – perhaps someone in your family or a friend – that is just in the way of your dreams? It reminds me of circus elephants.

Circus elephants never try to run away. You know why? Because they have been shackled down and chained in one place since the day they were born. These elephants grow up thinking, no matter what the circumstances, no matter how hard they try, they cannot escape. You just have to accept it and say, 'Well, I guess this is my life.'

When these elephants grow up, you don't even have to put a chain on their legs, because they're not going to try to run away.

Vivian Wijaya at the National Achievers Congress, Singapore.

So this baby elephant grew up working and working and working and working as a doctor, wearing a white coat. Until one day I find myself on the floor with blood gushing from my forehead.

I have finally collapsed from overworking …

That night, my best friend Irina came to visit me. Irina is a Russian girl. She had this big sad frown between her eyebrows as she said, 'Vivian, what happened to you?'

'Irina, I've been stressed for so many years. I work from morning until night, going through routine after routine without even knowing why, and earlier today there was a cancer patient in front of me and I didn't even give a damn. I just wanted to get the paperwork done so I could get two hours of sleep. Is that called life? Is that called adding value to other people's lives? I hate my life.'

After a few moments Irina spoke in a soft voice. 'Vivian, do you re-member that time we sneaked into that event to see Paulo Coelho, our hero, the writer of The Alchemist? You had a copy of the book in your hand and you asked him for an autograph, remember? And he wrote a personal message for you. I brought it with me. I think you should have a look and remember it.'

'A personal message from the writer of The Alchemist, for me?' I thought to myself.

'Dear Vivian, No matter what happens in life, always stay faithful to your dreams. Love Paulo.'

I hit me all at once that I hadn't done that. I went to medical school, I became a doctor, but I didn't try to realize my dream of becoming a successful comic book creator. You would have seen tears running

Veronica Tan

Vivian Wijaya onstage at the National Achievers Congress, Singapore.

down my face and at that moment I made a decision that I had to change.

I thought: 'I have to start living my dreams. I have to be me and I have to be authentic.'

Have you ever had that experience, where you have to be your authentic self? So you can be truly happy?

The years after that weren't easy for me because I had to learn to break out of these shackles. There were many more clashes with my family and people mocked me.

They said stuff like: 'You are trying to break into the teenage market when you're over 30? Are you kidding?'

'You're Indonesian. Come on, you're not even Japanese! Your Japanese language level is like that of a primary school student. And you're trying to write a bestselling comic in Japan? That's very realistic.'

'Even if you master your Japanese, they pick one in a million people. How special do you think you are?'

There are always moments of doubt and these voices seem loud. They're louder than this little voice inside of me that says, in Paolo's voice, 'No matter what happens in life, always stay faithful to your dreams.'

But slowly, little by little, things started to change. First I started winning comic competitions. Next I got a job as an assistant apprentice to a bestselling Manga comic author. Then came the big turning point in my life, when I finally made my professional debut as a comic book creator in one of Japan's most competitive magazines.

Suddenly I find myself rubbing shoulders with all these important people in the industry and then I get this media attention. I get TV interviews and then talk shows and even Fortune magazine did a whole article about me. They start calling me something new, an entrepreneur. What's that? Nobody has ever called me an entrepreneur before. I guess they mean I'm a risk-taker. I guess I am.

A year later, among 4,000 other delegates, I find myself in the National Achievers Congress 2013 in Singapore. Andy Harrington took to the stage and my life took another turn when he said, 'Why do you try so hard all your life to fit in when you were born to stand out?'

Then it hit me as I thought, 'Maybe there are other people like me. People who also feel shackled down and chained by this invisible chain as

I had been. Perhaps I can help them. Maybe I can help them achieve their dreams too.'

Then I joined Andy's Public Speakers University and his Professional Speakers Academy, where I learned to put a message together and package my knowledge so that I could teach it to many people at the same time on stage and online, and help them achieve their dreams.

And now I find myself, one year later, standing on stage in front of 5,000 people at the National Achievers Congress, sharing my story alongside Nick Vujici, Brendan Burchard, Les Brown and even Andy Harrington himself.

So in closing, please remember: there are no shackles on your legs. No matter what happens in life, always stay faithful to your dreams.

*This chapter's resource is to watch a video recording of a live performance of the first few minutes of one of my presentations as I position the audience, my subject and myself as an expert. It's on **www.passionintoprofit.info** and you'll find it under the heading 'Positioning yourself as the "go to" expert'.*

In a nutshell

- *Your personal story should position you as a trusted source of information.*

- *Your story should also provide a valuable lesson.*

- *Stories must not be told, they must be relived.*

- *Centre a story on a challenge you overcame to become who you are.*

- *Tell your story mostly through dialogue, not narration.*

_"_

In the information age ...

... content is king!

_"_

CHAPTER 5

PRODUCING WORLD-CLASS CONTENT

A re you brilliant at what you do? Do you have a natural gift, or have you honed your talent through hours of dedication and practice? Interestingly, being good at something does NOT necessarily mean you'll naturally know how to pass on your wisdom, knowledge and knowhow to others.

Great performers are often good 'in the moment', and their skills have become unconscious to the point they no longer need to think about it. Consider that most adults have known for many years how to drive a car on the road. The skill is now so automatic that while driving they can have a conversation, listen to music, think through their problems, shave or put on their make-up! But regardless of how competent you are at driving, it doesn't automatically follow that you can easily teach someone else how to drive.

In the flow, but *NOT* in the know

Many people are brilliant when they work with a person face-to-face. They come to life, switch on, become highly intuitive and seem to magically find the right answers for people. They are in the flow, or in the zone, and tap into their innermost wisdom to draw upon whatever experience they have. However, put these people in front of a piece of paper and ask them to describe how they do what they do and they go blank, seemingly losing their confidence and their natural flow.

Have you ever attended a seminar or workshop and felt overwhelmed by the speaker giving too much detail too quickly? Maybe you experienced the information as disjointed and poorly sequenced, leaving you feeling somewhat confused? Perhaps the content was so broad and conceptual you didn't really learn anything?

If you want to position yourself as an expert authority, you'll need to sit down and extract your knowhow. Ideally, you want to synthesize all your knowledge into a comprehensive system that can be taught to others as a step-by-step series of instructions of what to do and how to do it.

At the outset you won't need to decide if the content you'll produce will be something that your audience will read like in a book, ebook or manual. You don't need to know if they will hear it through an audio programme, and you don't yet need to commit to delivering it live in a workshop.

Here's why. Because before you do anything else you must first create …

A solution framework

A solution framework gives your audience a map of how to get from where they are to where they want to be. It gives them the big picture of the journey ahead and a way to navigate through the myriad of twists and turns by the most direct route.

You can think of a solution framework as a model, a system, a blueprint, a map, a template, a diagram or a matrix. Without one, your audience is sure to be lost, because they won't be able to easily follow your advice and your content will be too loose.

However, this is where most people fail in our industry. Coaches, consultants, gurus, mentors, speakers and seminar leaders want to make a difference and become the next Tony Robbins, Robert Kiyosaki or Brian Tracy. But they never do the work of sitting down and *creating their own unique solution framework* that sets them apart from the rest.

Being seen as an expert authority

Successful thought leaders create their own systems to explain how to get from pain to gain. They detail the steps required to climb the obstacles preventing people from being able to move forward easily on their own.

I believe many well-known experts have become so because of their solution frameworks. Would Stephen Covey's work be so well known without his book *The Seven Habits of Highly Effective People*? Would Robert

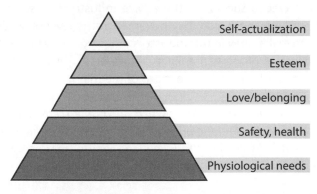

Abraham Maslow's Hierarchy of Needs

Kiyosaki have helped millions of people without the Cash Flow Quadrant? Would we even talk about the work of Abraham Maslow without his famous Hierarchy of Needs? Creating a solution framework for your ideas becomes the basis of what you stand for. Your ideas, principles and beliefs can be built into your model. Every strategy, tactic or action step that teaches your audience what to do and how to do it should stem from it.

A model or a framework should simplify complex ideas, essentially making it easier to learn step-by-step. However, interestingly, and more importantly, having a solution framework will also make sharing and teaching the material easier too. But perhaps most importantly, it will make your content teachable beyond yourself.

This is crucial, because you may not want to always be the one to deliver the content. To grow your business, you may want to train other trainers to teach your courses for you. But if you haven't systemized your content and just show up and do your thing, you may find it impossible for someone else to come in and replicate what you do ...!

Where the real money is made

There is a secret to success in the advice industry. It is so important that without knowing it, you may never reach the level of success you deserve. The real money in this industry comes from creating and leveraging intellectual property. Intellectual property rights are the legally recognized exclusive rights to creations of the mind.

'Under intellectual property law, owners are granted certain exclusive rights to a variety of intangible assets, such as musical, literary and artistic works, discoveries and inventions, words, phrases, symbols, and designs.'

The Seven Habits of Highly Effective People would not have been the global success it became if Stephen Covey had to deliver the content himself. Instead, Franklin Covey has trained and licensed more than 45,000 individuals to teach the principles of the *Seven Habits*. None of this would be possible without the original framework contained within the book.

Create once, leverage forever

The beauty of designing and developing your own framework is that once it's created, it becomes the foundation of everything you do. When you write your book, each chapter is based on a part of your framework. In your 90-minute introductory talks you teach and tease the audience with your framework, so that they feel compelled to take your advanced training to know more. Each segment of your advanced training is based on a part of your framework, allowing people to go deeper into the nuances of the material. All of your information-based products, whether audio or visual, will have your overarching framework at their core.

The mind is like a computer

When downloading a file onto your PC or Mac, you need somewhere to store it if you are going to keep it and be able to use it again. The best way to achieve this is to store each file in a folder with similar items. This folder may in turn be a subfolder of another folder, and so on. Why am I telling you this? Because the mind is like a computer. Your audience needs you to organize your content into a neat system so that as they learn it, they know where everything fits in.

Think of your model as like a putting together a jigsaw puzzle. The picture on the box gives you an image of what success looks like. The straight-edged pieces help form the framework. The individual pieces can be sorted into the parts of the overall picture that they represent.

We intrinsically know that completing a jigsaw puzzle is easier when we chunk the task in this way, and that is precisely what you need to do when organizing your content for our audience.

At my Public Speakers University we devote a major part of the first day to the teaching, designing and development of what I call your Unique Branded Solution™, or UBS for short. I love it when the penny drops for people who for years may have been struggling to position themselves as experts when they see how it's done. The beauty of creating a solution framework is that it stands up on its own and begins to make the intangible (your ideas) look tangible.

Let's now take a look at how to go about putting together your UBS.

1. Revisit your audience's problems

Remember that your solution must solve a problem or a group of problems for your audience. This means that you must *know your audience*, as we discussed in Chapter 3. Otherwise, you may end up creating a solution, only to find it's *not* the specific solution your audience needs.

For audiences who want to learn to become world-class presenters, I created a solution framework called the Jet Set Speaker System™. It's the foundation for the material delivered at the Public Speakers University and mastered through the Professional Speakers Academy. But before I created any of this, I first had to decide which problems my audience was experiencing and needed a solution for.

Specifically, my audience is made up of coaches, consultants, authors, managers, entrepreneurs, healers, therapists and industry experts, or just those people wanting to get a message out into the world. I discovered there were four big areas where they were not successful and needed advice. They needed to have:

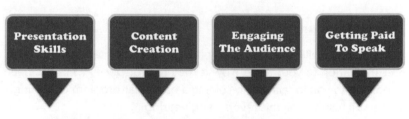

The four problems that my Jet Set Speaker System solves.

- Better presentation skills

- A way of structuring their content

- The ability to engage an audience and

- Most importantly, how to increase their income and get paid more for sharing their knowledge and knowhow.

2. Research

No matter what your subject matter is, it's likely there are already other experts out there with something to say on the topic. Rather than blindly putting your own content together, it is first sensible to take a look at what is being taught by the established people in your industry.

I suggest making a big list of all their points of wisdom. Have a look at how they lay out their knowledge and knowhow. Do they have a model or framework that helps them to get their points across? How have they ordered and sequenced their content? Does it follow a logical flow? At this point, don't evaluate their content – just write it down and collect their salient points.

3. Reverse engineer

No doubt you will have personally had some successes and some fail-ures in relation to your topic. Now is the time to specify what has been important to you in relation to solving a particular problem or getting a successful result. I call this reverse engineering.

When I created the Jet Set Speaker System I looked at each of the four areas my audience wanted answers:

- Presentation skills

- Content creation

- Engaging the audience

- Getting paid to speak.

I studied what I had done that had worked for me and got me to the point of speaking to thousands of people alongside well-known names like Richard Branson, Bill Clinton and Donald Trump. I watched video re-cordings of my performances to see what I was doing so I could become even more conscious of my skill and teach it to others as a part of my solution framework.

4. Organize

By now you will know the problems you need to solve for your audience. You will also know what other experts do to get results, what you do that gets you results and you'll have a big list with lots of points of wisdom.

However, at the moment, you have some great points that are unorgan-ized. Essentially you have lots of pieces to various jigsaw puzzles, so now it's time to chunk, order and sequence. This means assigning each point to one of the problems you are trying to solve and then categorizing your points into folders and subfolders just like you would if it was information on your computer.

Your aim is to have three to seven top-level points of wisdom (folders) that contain within them a number of specific points of wisdom (subfolders). These potentially contain the most detailed of all instructions (files) on how to do achieve a particular task.

This gives you three layers to your solution and this is the key to a great framework. The top layer provides general direction on what to focus on. The second layer tells your audience what to do and the third layer gives them the very specific instructions, including all the nuances on how to do it.

5. Assemble

Now at this point you have to turn what is essentially a collection of bullet points into a solution framework that is world-class, will stick in your audience's mind and position you as the 'go to' expert in your industry.

Taking your points of wisdom in each layer, you must now assemble them into one of three structures:

- **Acronym**, where the first letter of each point together spells a word.

- **Alliteration**, where the first letter of each point starts with the same letter.

- **Shape or structure**, where each point is built around a shape or solid object.

Here is an example of an acronym-based system called the Stress Free Speaker S.Y.S.T.E.M. to teach my audiences great presentation skills:

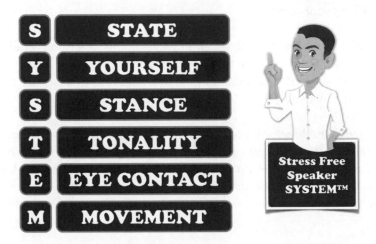

S	STATE
Y	YOURSELF
S	STANCE
T	TONALITY
E	EYE CONTACT
M	MOVEMENT

Stress Free Speaker SYSTEM™

Here is an example of an alliteration-based system called the Tri-Summit Storytelling System™ to teach my audiences how to design, develop and deliver a well-crafted story.

S	SCENE
S	STARS
S	STRUGGLE
S	SUMMIT
S	SOLUTION
S	SEED

Tri-Summit Storytelling System™

Thousands of my students around the world are building their own UBS. Here's an example of one built by Sammy Blindell and Miles Fryer. Their company is called How to Build a Brand and because of this framework they are now well on the way to leading their industry.

Miles and Sammy's story

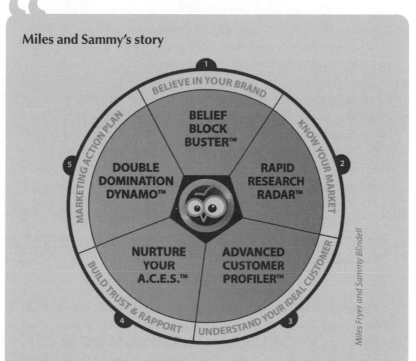

Miles and Sammy's shape based UBS.

Back in July 2013 we were running a successful brand and marketing agency in Leeds. With 12 expert staff, we helped our clients achieve great results. However, our passion meant that we worked so hard we became stressed and ill, and lacked a work-life balance. We were happy in work, but not happy in life. This was certainly not what we got into business for. So we had to make changes. We sold the agency and followed a new, far more exciting road. Yes, it was a risk – but when you believe in what you do so passionately, and it has the ability to change lives, it's a risk worth taking.

After attending Andy Harrington's Public Speakers University and, subsequently, graduating to the Professional Speakers Academy, we discovered a much better way to deliver our knowledge and expertise on a massive scale ... such that we can reach thousands of our ideal customers more effectively than ever before.

As brand and marketing experts for more than 18 years, we knew about the power of brand positioning. Now with this extra jigsaw piece we were able to see the bigger picture for both our business and the businesses we supported worldwide. This success is greatly attributed to the system Andy taught us – how to package our knowledge into a system and present it with impact to a much wider audience.

Our business transformed within six weeks of attending the Public Speakers University and the ripple effect continues to positively enhance our reputation, our bank balance, our lives and – more importantly – the lives of those we love around us.

We learned so much at the Public Speakers University that by implementing the strategies we learnt, our turnover increased by more than 400 per cent. We stopped exchanging all our time for money and instead turned our knowledge into online products that made us residual income. As a result, our consultancy prices sextupled! The hours we spent in the business reduced dramatically and as a wonderful added bonus, our lives are so much richer because we now get to spend time doing what we love with the people we love.

Through systemizing our knowledge and knowhow coupled with our greatly enhanced presentation skills, we now present our B.R.A.N.D. Accelerator Marketing programme to a much larger audience. Wow!

What a difference! Our customers are so impressed by how easy it is to understand the brand and marketing process using our programme that our conversion tripled immediately. We have since increased the price of our programme five times because demand for it is so high and our customers still tell us that it's too cheap for what it gives them!

What's more, because the skills we learned are transferrable from presenting on stage to presenting on video and webinars, our business has now gone global. We have customers in the UK, France, Holland, Spain, Australia, the USA and South Africa already.

And here's the thing ... we launched our new business with just the two of us in October 2013 and within six months we were earning more than we were as an agency of 13 people. All that without staff, without expensive glass-fronted offices, free from stress, no more long hours, working wherever we want in the world and, most importantly, with the freedom to choose life over work!

Miles and Sammy presenting their Unique Branded Solution.

6. Name it …!

Your goal in building a solution framework is to create a UBS. It's unique because you created it, and if you have followed the steps correctly, it should be a brilliantly systemized solution. All we need now is to brand your solution by giving it a catchy sounding name. Your name should describe what the solution does or the result it produces. We also want to give it a name that makes it sound more solid and tangible.

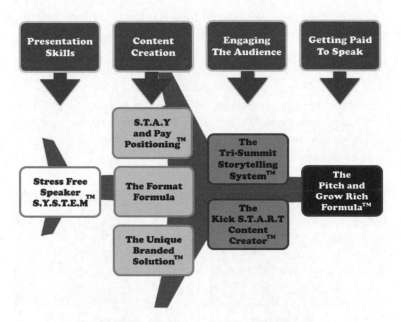

The Jet Set Speaker System and all its subsystems

The Jet Set Speaker System shown here is the high-level layer of *my* solution framework. At the top are four problems to be solved. Underneath are seven subsystem solutions. Each of the seven subsystems are further frameworks that go into the finer detail of WHAT to do with another layer underneath giving instructions and HOW to do it.

Diving deeper

Creating and crafting *your* UBS gives you the positioning of an expert authority and provides you and your audience with a structure. The next step is to flesh out this structure with content that widens your audience's understanding. The advantages of first organizing your ideas into a framework are that you will never have to write the script of a speech word-for-word. From now on, when you deliver a keynote presentation, or a segment of content within your workshop, you have a structure that allows freedom of expression, while still remaining on track, on topic and on time.

Those presenters who try to write down their content and memorize it word for word are making life very hard for themselves. Whenever I see a presenter trying to remember a script, they are inevitably nervous. Even the ones who pull it off have zero stage presence because their attention is internal (thinking about words) rather than external (focusing and connecting with their audience).

Conscious v. unconscious delivery

Those presenters who memorize their content are trying to do something that is unnatural. Perhaps you haven't thought about this before, but speaking is an unconscious skill. When was the last time you thought about what you were going to say word for word before you said it? This type of talk is for politicians who stand behind lecterns delivering canned presentations.

So just how do you create content that is easily recalled and delivered, with real passion and power to boot?

Let me ask you a question ...

If you were to eavesdrop on a debate between two people discussing a topic they both felt passionate about, you would discover something startlingly simple about the structure of their conversation: they will either be making a STATEMENT or asking a QUESTION.

Now this might seem obvious, but I have an important revelation to make regarding this and most presentations, and here it is: 'Most speakers only make statements and forget to ask questions!'

A great presentation should NOT sound like a presentation. Instead, it should sound like a conversation. The only difference is that the presenter is asking AND answering the questions.

The easiest way to create your content is to think like your audience and consider what your audience would ask you (if they could) at any given moment of your presentation. Then simply ask this question rhetorically and then answer the question yourself. In so doing you would have educated your audience and your answer may have now raised another question in their mind, so what do you do?

Pose this new question (again rhetorically) and your answer provides even more content, which deepens their understanding further.

Why is asking rhetorical questions vital to a great presentation? Simply put, this style of presentation makes people think and not just learn.

Thinking to learn v. listening to learn

Whenever you pose a rhetorical question and pause for a few moments before answering, your audience will attempt to answer the question in their head. Much of the time they will be wrong or have no answer, but what this does is create interest in the topic and make them more curious.

Why is that? I'll tell you …

Because questions are evaluations, causing people to think for themselves and not just be spoon-fed information. A rhetorical question
also opens up a space for the answer to be stored in the minds of the
audience, and furthermore gives them an opportunity to relate to other
answers already given.

This style of presentation will also have a conversational tone and feel to
it (even though the audience aren't actually speaking). The huge advantage of this is that your audience will stay alert and attentive for much
longer periods and therefore learn and retain your information much
better.

Questions are very hard to ignore. Presenters that intersperse their content with well-placed questions are way more engaging than a speaker
who just rattles off statement after statement in a lecturing style.

Get agreement along the way

Having created your solution framework – your UBS – each point you
make should relate directly back to it in some way. If you are making
each point well, you'll be validating each point you make – more about
how to do this in a minute. Make sure that once you have made your
point, you get an agreement from your audience. In doing so you begin
to validate your entire framework as a reliable and useful system of what
to do and how to do it.

Having made your point all you need to do is simply make a statement
or ask a question such as 'Raise your hand if that makes sense to you',
'Raise your hand if you understand' or 'Do you agree with me? Yes or no.'

Most presenters often overlook this technique of getting small agreements along the way. They often fear a negative response from the audience or worry that people won't participate, so they don't 'check in' with
their audience. This is a BIG mistake.

Feedback is the breakfast of champions

Without 'checking in' with your audience you will have little way of knowing how well you are doing and if your audience is 'with you' or not. The chances are they will be. They will raise their hand or say yes to your question and, in doing so, they'll be in agreement with you. Remember that you want to influence this audience to follow your advice and make a change. By getting small agreements along the way, you'll be one step closer to the bigger agreement of implementing your advice and potentially hiring you or buying the product or service you provide.

Now you may ask, 'But Andy, what if my audience doesn't usually respond and I don't think they will raise their hands or agree by saying yes?' It's a fair question, but first – how do you know until you just do it? Also, to overcome this, simply create a pre-frame at the beginning of your talk saying that you will be asking your audience to respond to you as you need feedback to know your message is making sense.

Stop *just* giving information

So far in this chapter we have discussed the huge benefits of creating your solution framework as a UBS to position yourself as an authority while making your content follow a logical system. This way of putting your message together is vital to your long-term success in this game. It helps you to give a concrete feel of substance to your massage. This is predominately teaching the left side of the brain, which processes information in a logical, ordered and sequenced way. We have also talked about the use of questions to open up your audience and make your style more conversational.

However, just dealing in left-brain logic is not going to make you a world-class influencer. Here's why: it's not enough to simply *inform* people. You must go one stage further and *transform* them too.

Essentially, you must ...

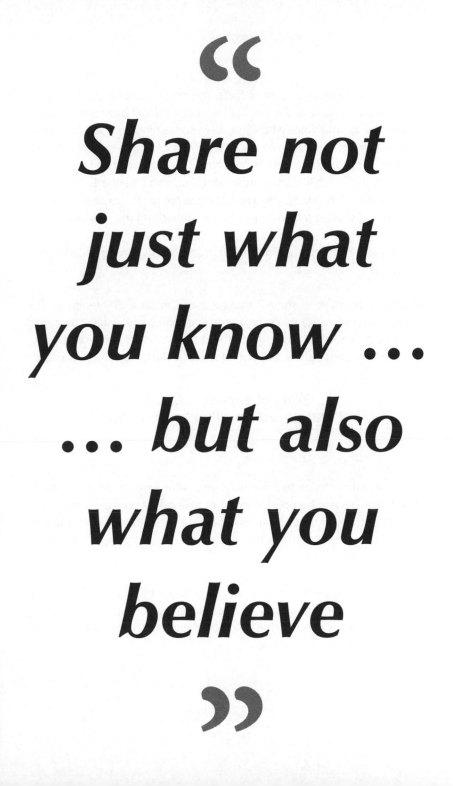

"

Share not just what you know ...

... but also what you believe

"

Don't just give people content or facts. You must interpret the facts and share your perspective and beliefs. Think about the difference in the level of conviction in your voice when you share something you believe versus just sharing what you know. It's a subtle difference with a massive impact and all great speakers do it. Think of some of the greatest speakers of all time: Winston Churchill, Martin Luther King Jnr, John F. Kennedy, Mahatma Gandhi. If you listen closely, you'll realize these are great speeches because the speaker is sharing a deep conviction in something they believe.

Now, this brings me to one undeniable truth. Not everyone will like you. Get over it!

It takes real courage to share a message and make a difference to the people in your family, your community, your company, your country, or the world. It's important to know that not everyone will agree with your ideas, or share your beliefs. But don't let that deter you from your path.

'You got enemies? Good. That means you stood up for something.'
Eminem

You cannot afford to be too 'vanilla' if you want to succeed in the guru industry. You have to be opinionated because people are paying you for your perspective, so you better have one …! The easiest way to make a name for yourself is to attack the status quo of what people believe to be true in your industry.

Be commentating on the current way of doing things and pointing out how the world has changed, you begin to create an opening for your new and better way and in doing so, further position yourself as an authority and an expert.

Molly Burr

Find your authentic voice – make a stand and attract your posse.

People learn best by association

Have you ever been in a seminar or a meeting and been confused or overwhelmed? I know I have. I believe even the most technical subjects can be explained in simple terms, provided the teacher links the unknown (technical content) to the known (something the audience is already familiar with).

The human brain learns best by association. When we discover something for the first time, we search for what it is 'like'. When we find a match, we have a feeling of familiarity and make a step change in our understanding. There are three primary ways to associate your points of wisdom.

1. Associate with a universal experience

You could choose to liken your point to an everyday experience that most of your audience could relate to, such as various aspects of driving a car, perhaps – changing gear, looking in the mirrors or applying the brakes. The universal experience acts like a metaphor and accelerates and deepens the understanding of your audience.

*Now visit **www.passionintoprofit.info** and watch a video recording of a live performance where I liken our ability to spot or miss opportunities to driving a car. You'll find it under the heading 'Producing world-class content'.*

2. Associate with a story

An anecdotal story is a fantastic way of helping your audience to learn. You could tell a story from your own life or someone you know – perhaps even someone in the public eye. Your story acts as evidence that the point you are making is valid and true in the real world.

Here's a short story I use to deepen the audience's understanding of a point I make in my Public Speakers University.

Leaders do what is right, not what is easy

Have you ever been faced with a difficult decision where it was easier to not speak up rather than telling the truth?

If you had worked at Churchill Insurance in February 1997 you would have been invited to gather for a five-minute meeting in the atrium in the middle of the sales floor. It's a meeting I knew was coming and I was prepared for the repercussions that would ensue once I had 'upset the apple cart'.

Having worked for Churchill Insurance for seven years, this was my brief farewell meeting. I was due to leave the relative safety of the company with the view to starting my first business. I clutched my gift of Dolce & Gabbana aftershave and made my announcement.

'Thank you to all of you for the wonderful years we have spent together working for Churchill, but today I am leaving. And the reason it's time for me to move on is because I believe I have outgrown this place.'

Well, you could have heard a pin drop. I was told later that people were gossiping and saying, 'Who does he think he is?' and 'What an arrogant idiot.'

The reason I said it was firstly because it was true but also because I believe you cannot succeed with your feet planted in two worlds. You see, over the previous seven years I had watched people leave Churchill to start something new, only to see them return and ask for their job back when the going got tough and their new venture hit a roadblock.

I knew if I made that bold statement, there would be no way back for me. I burned the bridge so that there would be no easy way back from the moment I said what I did.

But here's what's interesting. There were five people in that meeting who over the next 18 months came to work for my new company. They all tripled their income and have gone on to run their own successful companies, generating revenues into the multi-millions.

> *So what's something you need to say? Is there something you need to do? Do you need to end something that is no longer serving you? Do you need to commit to someone or something that you have been putting off?*
>
> *I believe this ...*
>
> *Leaders do what is right, not what is easy. What is easy is to go with the flow – but remember that the gentle flow of the stream may become a current you can't control. One day you may end up heading for a waterfall because you didn't do the right thing when you had the chance.*

3. Associate with an activity

The final way you can deepen your audience's understanding of your point is to have it participate in an activity. Many people learn best by doing, so why not create an exercise or a game so that it can they experience the point you are making?

One of my favourite games is Knotty Problem.

The whole group stands in a circle and holds hands – all except one person, who will be the leader. The group then proceeds to create a giant human knot by moving in multiple directions while keeping hold of each other's hands.

After a minute, everyone stops. It's then the job of the leader to work out how to undo the knot and instruct people how to move to achieve this. This approach takes several minutes, but finally the group will be back in the same circle that they started in.

Then the exercise is repeated, except you are the leader. When everyone is tied up in the human knot, you simply say: 'Well I think since you got yourself into the knot, you probably know the best way to resolve it. So would you please go back to how you were without letting go of your hands?'

Magically, within less than ten seconds, the group is back in its original circle. Most managers try to solve problems themselves without empowering their teams.

Now I make my point.

When it comes to high-performance ...

'Teamwork makes the dream work.'

Ultimately, putting world-class content together takes time. But remember: you are creating your intellectual property, which will become an asset you will leverage over and over again for the rest of your life, and possibly beyond, for your family.

In a nutshell

- *Produce a solution framework for your ideas.*

- *Brand your solution by giving it a unique and catchy name.*

- *Use rhetorical questions for a conversational style.*

- *Don't just inform people – transform them too.*

- *Be controversial, be different and attack the status quo.*

- *Associate your points to things that people are already familiar with.*

CHAPTER 6

PRODUCTIZING YOUR KNOWLEDGE

This book is titled *Passion into Profit* because it teaches you how to help potentially millions of people to solve a problem, make a change, increase their results or generally improve their lives or business in some way. I therefore think it's only fair that in return you deserve to be hugely financially rewarded for your efforts. This means realizing the intrinsic value of what you have to offer and making a successful business to support you on your mission.

Passion into *BIG* profits

The great news about creating and building a business in the 'mentoring, coaching and advice-giving' industry is that you get to make money doing something you genuinely love. Consider how many people travel each day to their job or business to do work they have little or no passion for. For me, this is crazy – but I understand it, because for years I didn't recognize *my* value and settled for stacking shelves in a supermarket!

I believe that if you do something you love, you'll do it a lot.

If you do it a lot, you'll get very good at it.

If you get very good at it, you'll be better than most.

If you're better than most, you'll probably be able to charge premium fees.

Products *and* services

To make money and thrive, every business has to sell *something* for a profit. The *something* that is sold will either be a product or a service. The beauty of the 'expert' industry is that you'll be able to create and offer both …!

Essentially, as experts passing on wisdom we are the creators of content, the inventors of information, the suppliers of strategies, the providers of perspective, the mentors with maps. Our 'how to' information solves problems and reduces the time required and stress incurred by our audiences, saving them the need to figure it out by themselves through trial and terror …!

We first find out what answers people need. Then we go to work to structure our highly valuable knowledge and knowhow in such a way that they can access those answers, implement our advice and get the results they want.

Packaging the genie within

You can 'package' your knowledge and knowhow either through an information product you create and produce, or through a service such as a workshop, a seminar or a face-to-face coaching consultancy or mentoring session. Products are fantastic for reaching out and helping people who you may never meet in person. I love the idea that someone in the world has the chance to massively improve the quality of their lives because of one of my products.

Right now I am thrilled to bits you are reading this book (product). I'm jazzed that, as every chapter unfolds, I have the opportunity to connect with you and ignite a spark within, which I hope and believe will become an eternal flame of desire to make your mark on this world, help others and leave a lasting legacy.

Why products?

Products are also brilliant for your audience, as it can gain access to your material without the physical effort, higher cost and availability to come to a live event or a personal session. Your audience can learn at its own pace and from the comfort of the home, or in the car as they drive around. As Brian Tracy always said, they can turn their car into a university on wheels!

Your business will flourish better with products, because you work once to create them and you get paid over and over again each time a new customer buys them. This allows you to build a business that is leveraged and scalable. This means it doesn't matter that there are only 24 hours in a day because you do not have to deliver the service over and over again personally – the information product you created does the work for you …!

Why services?

Services in the form of live events such as workshops, seminars, retreats and mastermind programmes give your audience a chance to immerse themselves in the learning experience. They give your audience an opportunity to meet and greet like-minded people with similar problems, goals, dreams and aspirations. It gives them a chance to meet you in person so that they can 'hear it from the horse's mouth', as it were.

The benefit of live events is that you can serve lots of people in one event, as your only limitation is the size of room you hire. Typically, to conduct the event, you will hire a conference room in a hotel within easy reach of your audience. When your events get bigger, you can hire bigger venues such as exhibition and conference centres.

I started out delivering events in small conference rooms in hotels, as my audiences were small. My first three-day weekend event had just 26 paying people. The exciting prospect is that, by following the advice throughout this book, you may also be able to scale up to huge venues and speak in front of audiences of thousands too.

To begin with you will need a short signature talk that will both teach and tease people into wanting advanced training. My personal preference

Holding my daughter Amelia at the end of an event in Singapore.

Gagan Arora

Just before we open the door at the Public Speakers University in a London hotel.

is a three- or four-day seminar as I can deliver more than my audience expects.

If you do this too, you'll create an army of raving fans who'll become a walking, talking advert for your training programmes.

Far too many coaches, mentors and consultants only offer their advice on a one-to-one basis. This is a BIG mistake. Don't get me wrong; doing one-to-one work should still be part of your services. But here's the critical distinction:

'Make personal sessions the *last* thing people buy from you, *not the first.*'

As someone who wants to be seen and known as an authority in your chosen field, you'll want to give people a chance to learn from you through a product or through a group training seminar first. Why? Because it's highly leveraged.

It stands to reason that if I am conducting a one-day seminar with 3,650 attendees I am being 3,650 times more time-efficient than if I worked with them all one-to-one, which would take me ten years to do. Of course, this also means that I am making the same money (less a few additional costs) in one day as I would otherwise make in a decade!

But that's not the only reason to offer a product or a seminar first. Think about the limitations of only offering one-to-one mentoring or coaching. Consider that in the beginning of your relationship with a potential client, they will be naturally sceptical about whether you can help them or not. If the only option is having a personal one-to-one with you, they'll feel they are taking a risk in trying you out. Because of this you'll most likely have to keep the cost of your one-to-one sessions right down to attract business.

However, when you produce a low-priced product, you give your customer a chance to gain *some knowledge and knowhow* for a small investment. As they consume the material, they will begin to hold you in higher regard, and will start to see you as the expert authority you are. You will have built a relationship of trust and credibility. You can then follow-up with further automated marketing and convert them into a higher-paying customer. (More about this in Chapter 7, 'Promoting Yourself and Your Services'.)

Live events

A live event gives you the same benefits but magnified. When your client is sitting in an audience as you deliver your advice from stage, they'll almost certainly hold you in even higher regard, and you'll be positioned in their mind as even more of an authority. This happens because of social proof. All those other people in the audience demonstrate that *many* people want your advice, not just them.

All of this is vital to the success you will enjoy in this business. If you offer one-to-one sessions as your first or only service to help people, you will be de-positioning yourself by making yourself too available too early in the relationship and for too cheap a price …!

But if, having bought your products and attended a few of your seminars, someone wants a one-to-one with you, do you think they would be willing to pay a much higher price? You bet they will would – in fact, they expect it!

Today I still do one-to-one sessions but I charge £20,000 for a single session with me. Charging a premium for *your* one-to-one advice will serve you in a number of ways:

1. Only serious people will book you

The very last thing you want to do is work with non-committed people. They will drain your time and energy. When someone invests a decent amount of money to work with you, they are focused and typically at a point where making a change is a must. There is a much higher probability that they will implement your advice rather than just turn up to the sessions and go through the motions.

2. You will attract amazing people to work with

When you charge a premium fee, a funny thing happens. People will naturally believe you are unique and special. Now, understand for every customer out there that only wants to buy the cheapest solution, there are also a whole host of people who only want to buy the best (most expensive) solution. You know that has to be true, or luxury goods such as Rolex, Louis Vuitton, Ferrari, Aston Martin and Porsche wouldn't exist. So who are the people who want to buy the best solution?

Often you will attract high net worth individuals, C-level executives of corporations or even celebrities. I have had the privilege of working with and speaking alongside many of the great movers and shakers of the world. Do you think they would be comfortable hiring me if I only charged £500 a day? Remember, price itself is the ultimate positioning tool. In addition, when you attract these types of clients your business will expand, because what sets apart successful people is their focus and desire to build networks. Once you work with one celebrity, you often get the opportunity to work with many more.

3. You will raise your game

In order to justify a high price for one-to-one coaching, you will need to provide a world-class solution and help your client to overcome their challenge and get the result they are looking for. Your service must be of high quality. Knowing this, you will become the best you can be. You'll attend more seminars and buy products to stay at the cutting edge. You'll work harder at improving your approach and the way you work. All this serves to make you even better, which may in turn enable you to raise your fees even more.

4. Your belief in you and your value goes up

If you charge too little for your one-to-one work, you may attract non-committed people. When they don't get results – not because you didn't advise them well, but because they failed to implement your advice – it may start to affect your belief in your ability. However, when you charge a premium and attract clients that are happy to pay your fees and thrilled with the results they get from implementing your advice something magical happens, your belief in what you are worth financially will rise.

I cannot underestimate the importance of this phenomenon. Our beliefs massively affect the amount of money we are worth. Do not make the mistake of charging too little – because when customers pay it, you'll start to believe that's what you are worth. You may get stuck at one level of income for the rest of your career.

5. You get paid more for doing less

The problem with offering your advice as a service is that you are essentially exchanging your time for money. It's essentially a job. Many people become a coach, mentor or consultant to break away from the corporate world. They want more control and more time-freedom – but if they are successful and get booked up, they will soon be back in the same boat, exchanging time for money. Of course, they will be doing something they love. But the business will never grow, because you can't scale a business based on one-to-one work.

Almost every new entrant into this industry produces a business that is upside down. They start with one-to-one then try a one-off seminar that they can't fill because their clients have already had a one-to-one session, so why would they pay for a 'one-to-many' experience? So the new entrant goes back to one-to-one sessions and dreams one day of producing an information product like a book or a set of CDs.

If you want to make it big and turn a passion into profit, you'll need to create a business that begins by offering an information product in written, audio or visual format. You then move to seminars or workshops, and then perhaps to small group mentoring, and finally to premium-priced one-to-one mentoring.

Times have changed for good

As you start to think about creating your own products and seminars, you may start to freak out and worry that you'll never be able to do it. Please relax. Throughout this book I will explain how to achieve all of this easily. Because you will have already created your UBS and your 'what to do' and 'how to do it' content around it, creating an information-based product is much easier than you might think.

When it comes to creating products, times have changed for good. In the past we creators had to book studio time (which was very expensive), go into a room and perform on demand to record our voice or stand in front of a video camera.

All of that has changed. Today, with the use of your PC or Apple Mac, you can produce a product in the comfort of your own home, at your own pace, that is as good in quality as anything produced in a studio.

Let's now take a look at the types of products and live events you could create for your audience ...

Audio programmes

If you are creating an audio programme, you have the choice of whether it should be delivered to your customer as physical CDs or as down-loaded MP3 files. If you are an Apple Mac user, simply use GarageBand, which comes free with every purchase of a Mac. If you own a PC running

Windows, use Audacity. Again, this is free software that you can download easily from the Internet.

Pictured above is one of my flagship products, called 'Breakthrough to the Life You Deserve'. It is a self-coaching course for those who want to overcome those mental barriers to success and making money while raising what they believe they are worth. It is an audio product made using GarageBand from the comfort of my own home, and it's helped change the lives of people all around the world.

Screen capture programmes

You could record an audio programme together with screen capture. Essentially, you put some slides together, hit record and the software records your voice while visually capturing whatever your screen is displaying.

This also means that an instructional product can easily be made this way, demonstrating to your audience what to do on your computer. If you are using an Apple Mac, I recommend downloading ScreenFlow from the Internet; if you are a PC person, you can download Camtasia.

The product featured above is called Winning Webinars and it teaches how to construct and deliver great webinars for the purposes of educating your audiences while providing an invitation for them to enrol in one of your live classes. I made it in three days using ScreenFlow, stopping and starting the record button while I occasionally stopped to eat, have a cup of tea, play with the kids or snuggle down with my wife!

Recording of a live event

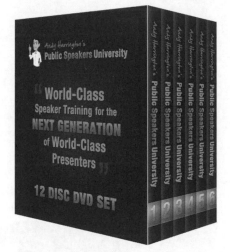

One of the mantras I am always drumming into my audiences is to make sure they capture all their live content whenever possible.

When you run a live event, I recommend having it recorded. By doing so, not only are you getting paid to deliver your live event, but you are also making a product that you can sell later.

Remember, some people won't be able to make it to the live event, or will prefer to learn in the comfort of their own home in their own time.

You can record the audio using a device connected straight into the sound desk running the audio at the event. Search on the Internet for one made by the company Roland. Alternatively, you could record the audio and the visuals, and produce a video product for people to have the 'best seat in the house', as if they were right there with you. The product shown is a video recording of my Public Speakers University live event where I teach people how to become a world-class presenter.

Instructional unpacking of a performance

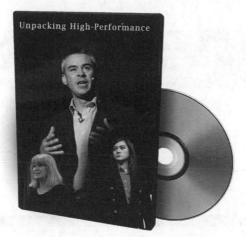

One of the types of products I love to create the most is one where I break a live performance down step-by-step. Your audience will benefit hugely from this type of product. Often, when someone is highly qualified at doing a particular skill, much of what they are doing is unconscious competence. This means that they don't have to think about what they are doing – it just comes naturally.

By recording yourself or someone else in the flow of their ability or performance, it is possible to demonstrate exactly what they are doing by pausing the action and adding a commentary over the top.

The product here is a live recording of one of my students having their onstage performance analysed. It was recorded using ScreenFlow to freeze-frame the action at key moments to describe their skills.

The beauty of this is you will be able to slow down your unconscious competence so that the audience becomes conscious of what you are doing. This can then be turned into a model of excellence and taught as steps to achieve mastery.

Online membership programmes

There is a special category of product that provides ongoing education for your audiences and so therefore ongoing (residual) income for you. If you want to create your ticket to retire young and retire rich, online membership programmes could help get you there.

With this type of product you create a modular training where you release new content each month that takes your audience one step closer to success. Typically your customer pays a monthly subscription and while they stay subscribed, they retain access to the already-released modules, as well as receiving each new module as it is released once a month.

This can sound like a lot of work, but in reality you record the content for each module in batches and produce many months' worth of content all in one day. You can also repurpose some footage of a live event and use this to create your modules.

The product shown here is my Professional Speakers Academy Online Coaching Programme, which breaks down how to design, develop and deliver world-class seminars, workshops and presentations.

Software tools

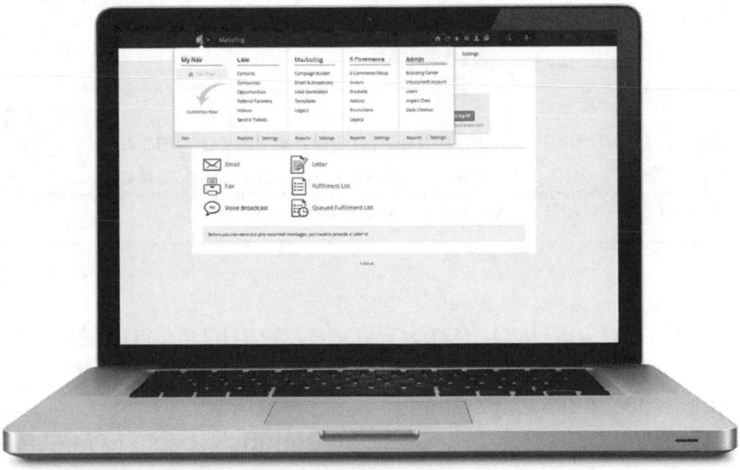

If you are technically minded perhaps you could create a software solution that solves a problem for people and their business.

The best way to sell your solution is to:

1 Educate your audience

2 Remind them of the problems they are facing

3 Educate them around the answers that are needed

4 Introduce and demonstrate your solution.

One such company, which provides fantastic customer relationship software, is Infusionsoft. Its software, called Infusion, helps me to collect and store customer information, organize all my marketing campaigns, and deliver messages to my audience so that I may serve them even better.

There are many suppliers of customer relationship management software on the market, but Infusion is the clear market leader. It allows me to run sophisticated marketing rather than just bombarding my audience with messages they don't want.

> *I highly recommend using Infusion from the very beginning of your entry into the expert industry. You can find out all about Infusionsoft at* ***www.infusionsoft.com***.

Comprehensive workshop-style training courses

Creating a live, multi-day training course that not only teaches people what to do but also gives them an opportunity to begin to implement your advice is where you showcase your real talents and abilities.

Workshop-style training courses that let the audience 'get its hands dirty' are very valuable, as many people who only learn theory at a seminar will often go back to their home or workplace but never start.

However when people start the process of implementation on the course, it also is a 'cause set in motion' and builds up momentum, making it much more likely they will continue to implement your advice once the event has finished.

Putting together a course requires you to devise modules so that it is easy for the audience to follow. Your content must be outlined, chunked and sequenced in a logical format. Far too many workshops leave their audiences confused and feeling inadequate – not because they are not intelligent people, but because the training was poorly designed.

The centrepiece of my training courses is the Public Speakers University, which teaches budding entrepreneurs, coaches, consultants, authors, trainers, speakers and would-be experts how to present like a professional, create world-class content, engage people and get paid to speak by learning how to pitch their products and services while delivering great education to their audiences.

High-end group mentoring programmes

Attending a live seminar gives your audience an immersion experience for a few days. But for those people in your audience who wish to attain mastery, you can create a group mentoring programme where people pay for a year or more and receive ongoing implementation advice and mentoring from you and your team. You can also create different tiers of membership that allow people to choose the level of commitment that best meets their budget and level of commitment. My high-end mastermind programme is the Professional Speakers Academy.

Multi-speaker events

Once you have begun making a name for yourself as someone who delivers great content AND has the ability to influence people, you may be invited to speak at a multi-day, multi-speaker conference. In these events you will typically present your 90-minute signature talk and invite people to enrol in an advanced course at the end of your talk. These events can be very lucrative as well as elevating your positioning when you speak alongside some of the best-known people in the industry.

Many speakers also create their own multi-speaker event where they become the promoter and fill the seminar room, and invite other well-known speakers to present. Some speakers will be paid a keynote fee while others will make money from selling their products and programmes.

Creating multiple formats

People often ask me, 'Andy, if I put all my ideas into a book or an audio programme, won't that mean people will not want to attend my work-shop or seminar?' This is a valid question, but here's what I always say in return:

'Have you ever bought a recording artist's album and then gone to see them live, singing exactly the same songs?' Then the penny drops.

People will buy an artist's album (product) and later go to their live con-cert (service); sometimes they will attend a live concert and then buy the album! People do this because they want to consume the material in different ways. I'm sure you'll agree that a live performance has a very dif-ferent feel compared with listening to a studio-recorded album. People attend live events for the experience to be moved both physically and emotionally as they dance, and they are also doing this with like-minded people. People buy the album because they want to take the artist home with them and listen to the songs over and over again in their car.

This industry – which I sometimes refer to as the 'expert', 'coaching', 'mentoring' or 'how to' industry – is no different. People who come to know, like and trust you through your products and programmes will want to attend your live events. People who attend your live events will want to take you home with them so they can listen to you over and over again in their car or watch you over and over again on their computer.

In a nutshell

- *Package your knowledge and knowhow to grow your business.*

- *Information products allow you to reach your audience more easily.*

- *People may want to read it, hear it, watch it or experience it live.*

- *Live events give your audience an immersion experience.*

- *Charge a premium for one-to-one sessions with you.*

Now you know how to create amazing content that informs and transforms, and can really help people to overcome a problem and get better results.

But what use is that if no one knows about you?

I think it's time we talked about …

CHAPTER 7

PROMOTING YOURSELF AND YOUR SERVICES

This chapter is where the rubber meets the road. Now we are going to take your expert positioning, together with your world-class information, products and services, and let the world know you exist and begin making a difference (and hopefully, a small fortune too).

It may sound like hyperbole but by following the advice in this chapter, you'll be able to start competing with the established players in your topic no matter how much of a celebrity they might be. You see, there is a process and a formula for success that I have been refining and updating for many years. Everything I'll teach you is based on actual campaigns I have run to sell my products and fill my own seminars and events.

How *NOT* to promote yourself and your services

It might seem strange to talk about what not to do, but I believe that learning what to avoid can be just as important as what to focus on. I am well qualified to tell you what NOT to do because I have done it all! My first attempt at promoting my events ultimately almost made me bankrupt. I made the mistake of using traditional marketing by placing quarter-page adverts in newspapers and 30-second adverts on radio. The problem with this approach is that while it will still bring in some customers, the cost of the advertising is so high and its effectiveness relatively low that it cannot be sustained long-term.

People like you and I are not giant conglomerate organizations with the luxury of huge budgets to spend on newspapers, magazines, radio, television and billboard posters. There is simply no point wasting our efforts on these forms of marketing, as they will not work – no matter how many people read that newspaper. The reason is because people are not reading the paper in the anticipation of reading your advert. You are paying a huge sum of money to get your advert in front of millions of people who simply have no interest in your service.

OK, so what should you do instead?

So what's the answer? Well, it's simple. We do the opposite. We get our marketing message in front of a much smaller number of clients with a high probability of being interested in what we are selling and we offer them an irresistible information product for free. Through this transaction we also capture their contact information, which enables us not only to send the free information products but also to begin a relationship.

Over a relatively short period of time we can establish our credibility and our expertise while building enough trust and belief in us they will happily pay for a higher-value information product or attend a live workshop or seminar.

Give and you shall receive

All of this type of marketing is built on the principle of giving first. If you do a one-off advert and try to sell to people straight away when you are not established in their mind as a trusted authority, you are not going to get many inquiries, let alone sales.

The new approach is to add value first by teaching, training or educating them around your subject. Your free gift could be an audio download, an online group master class, ebook, webinar, teleseminar or a series of training videos.

The beauty of this approach is that for the first time in history we can use 'pull marketing' strategies rather than 'pushing' our products and services on people who don't really want or need them. Push marketing is where we put out a message that says 'Buy my products' or 'Hire my services', and we try to convince someone to buy from us on the first contact.

As mentors, coaches and consultants we offer a solution that is often more personal than just functional. As such, it's vital to build up the relationship of trust first so that people choose to move towards us. If you were single and looking for a long-term, loving relationship, it wouldn't be an effective strategy to ask someone to come to bed with you within two minutes of meeting them. Even if you were successful, it's unlikely the relationship would last. In business we want to create longevity in our relationships with our customers so that we can continue to help them further whist increasing the lifetime value of our customers.

Turn the sales process into an educational process

The problem with traditional marketing is that it assumes everyone is ready to buy when you are ready to sell. This means that in order for you to make a sale, you have to perfectly time your marketing and advertising for each person.

Obviously this is impossible. Or is it?

The subtle shift here is to see people not as a potential client but as a student – someone to educate regardless of whether they buy or not. It's a game-changer when you turn the sales process into an opportunity for people to learn something valuable that begins to solve a problem they might be facing. Especially when it's free. Never try to sell without first adding value.

Creating the marketing machine

The key to all of this is to systemize and automate the process so that once it's set up, it requires little to no effort on your part and you have a steady stream of people buying your products and services or enrolling in your events. Although a few years ago this was difficult to pull off without huge investment and great technical skill, but the great news is that it is now it is possible even for people just starting out.

To promote yourself and your services you are going to need a few things in place first.

1. A contact management system

You'll need a system for collecting the contact information of each potential customer so that you can automatically run the campaigns I will describe later in this chapter. I personally use Infusion, but there are many others such as 1shoppingcart, iContact and AWebber, to mention just a few. I like Infusionsoft because it allows me to run sophisticated campaigns that track my customers' activity more accurately than the others.

*I highly recommend using Infusion from the very beginning of your entry into the expert industry. You can find out all about Infusion at **www.infusionsoft.com**.*

2. A merchant account

You'll need to get a merchant account so you can accept online credit card payments. Your bank can help you with this. Normally this involves filling out several forms, providing ID and jumping through a few hoops, but you need to do it. Alternatively you can use PayPal.

3. A high-quality product to give away for free

Because you want to create an ongoing relationship with your poten- tial customers, you are going to be giving away a free product so they get to know, like and trust you and your information. You want them to experience the quality of your content so that they will be hungry for more. Remember, if they love what you give them for free, they are much more likely to soon pay money for your entry-level product, service or workshop. This free 'product' should be delivered digitally as an ebook, audio, audio-visual or video-based programme.

Some experts give away a free seminar. You could do this too. The idea is for people to come to a two-hour event where, towards the end, you upsell to an advanced course.

When I first started out I used this approach and it worked well. However, a word of warning: you'll have a lot more cost, as you'll need to hire a venue and pay to hire sound equipment, as well as a technician to run it all. The other difficulty is getting the people who enrol on your free event to actually turn up and attend. Because it's a free event, they don't have much of a disincentive if they don't show. You'll find that, even with plenty of email reminders and even phone calls, your show-up rate is going to be about 50 per cent at best.

If instead as your free gift you offer a free audio, a recorded online master class or a video series that people can access immediately once they give you their contact information you'll be giving them instant gratification. The problem with a free live event is that they have to:

● Be available on the day of the event

● Travel

● Wait until the event itself to get the information.

I personally prefer to charge people for a live event once they have experienced my information through a free product that they can consume online first. This way, the event is not free (as it's a paid-for event), which means I haven't got to take the risk of putting on an event and hoping people will show up – I know they will, because they paid money to be there.

The only exception to this is if *someone else* is putting on a free or low-priced event and I am an invited speaker. I am happy for this to be part of my marketing strategy because I don't have the risk and the effort of putting the event on.

During these events I will normally present for 90 minutes and during my talk I will invite people to enrol in an advanced programme that my company runs – perhaps the Public Speakers University, or Passion into Profit. Typically I will share 50 per cent of the sales revenue with the promoter, but because enrolment in my live courses can run into the thousands, this is a good way to reach more people, fill our events and make a nice profit.

Speaking as a guest speaker at the National Achievers Congress in Amsterdam.

Okay, so let's assume you have your Infusion account in place, you've secured your merchant account and you have put together a brilliant information product you are going to give away for free. Now it's time to ...

Spend money to make money

As I have already said, you *could* blow your money on expensive adverts in a newspaper, or on radio or a magazine. But don't do this.

The best place to advertise is undoubtedly online. The Internet has been a game-changer for our industry, as it allows us to find and target the people who will see our marketing messages. Remember, the advantage of this is that you are not paying for people to see your adverts for something that they will never buy.

Now I imagine at this point that you may be concerned about spending money on advertising. But you must realize there is little to no point in having great products and services if no one knows about you. I understand your reservation. As someone who has spent thousands on an advert in a national newspaper with a readership of more than one million people and received zero inquiries, I know better than most that it can cost you a lot to find out what works and what doesn't.

However, what if I told you that there was a way of investing a very small amount of money and very quickly finding out if it is working and making you money? If it doesn't, you can turn the adverts off and it will cost you no more. However, when it does work, you can continue and potentially turn up your adverts too.

Imagine if you put a coin in a gaming machine and three coins came out the other end every time you play. Well, in this case, the coin going in is your investment into the first part of the machine, which is an online advertising platform like Google, Facebook or YouTube. The second part of the machine is your website, where people access your free content, and the three coins dropping out the other end represent your income a few days later from selling a high-value product, workshop or seminar.

Captivate attention

As I write this, I like YouTube as a primary source of adverts. (Although this could easily change as new platforms emerge.) It is not possible to go into fine detail here about every single step and nuance of using YouTube, but I will give you the overview.

Have you ever been on YouTube and clicked on a video and first had to watch an advert about something totally random? You most likely hovered over the 'Skip Ad' button, waiting for it to count down to zero, and then pressed it so you could get on with watching the video you wanted to watch in the first place, right? So your belief would understandably

Molly Burr

Create your own marketing machine.

be that using these 'pre-roll' or 'in-search' adverts, as they are known, wouldn't work. But you'd be wrong – very wrong.

The reason you clicked past the pre-roll advert is because it was most likely a random advert that did not relate in any way to the original video. It was also very obviously an advert to sell you something rather than information relating to something you were already interested in.

One of my main topics is teaching people like you how to become world-class speakers so you can share your message online, onstage or onscreen, and make money from it (hence the title of this book). Every day there are many people searching on YouTube for instructional videos on 'public speaking' or 'presentation skills', and some of these are better than others.

So what I do is this …

I select videos sharing information on public speaking with a relatively high number of views and place my pre-roll advert on it. This means my pre-roll advert will appear right before the original video about public speaking. Now, because my video promises great free information if they visit my website, every day many people click on the link in my advert and are redirected to my website. Hey presto! I've attracted a new visitor.

The results of your adverts can be recorded and measured so that you know exactly which adverts are producing the best results. The beauty of advertising platforms like YouTube and Facebook is that you can have your adverts only show to certain people depending on many factors, including for example where they live.

An example of a pre-roll or in-search advert on YouTube.

Remember: YouTube is just one example of the kind of advertising plat-forms available online. I like YouTube because it's video-based, which gives me (as an advertiser) the greatest opportunity to engage all the senses of my audience to inspire them to go to my website, where I can give away my product for free and start a long-term relationship.

Years ago you would have had to spend a fortune on TV advertising to get this kind of advert in front of people. Even if you could afford it, your audience was untargeted and they couldn't click a link on the TV – and even if they could, there would be no website as the Internet wasn't invented yet!

Remember, I was watching late-night television back in 2002 when Tony Robbins' 30-minute infomercial appeared. I'm not sure how much it cost to make and broadcast, but it was Tony's only option to spread his video message far and wide at that time. Of course, Tony now also uses the latest strategies for reaching out to help people, but I'm sure glad he reached out through TV all those years ago or I would not be writing this book and you wouldn't be reading it!

Perhaps this is a good moment to stop, reflect and remind ourselves what we are doing here. Yes, we are marketing to get our brand and our message out there and obviously make money. It's good to make money and it's only right and fair that you should be rewarded financially for your efforts. But always remember there are other rewards too. Knowing that you have helped someone to transform their life or results is surely the most valuable reward of all.

Personally I keep a file of all the letters, emails, posts, comments and cards where people have thanked me for reaching out and sharing my message. Don't get me wrong, the money is nice – but I believe the feeling of knowing you made a difference in someone's life is the real currency of behind why we do what we do.

Here's a story from Cheryl Chapman, who attended my events and changed her life to the extent that she ultimately became one of my international trainers. Who knows – maybe you'll be next?

"

Cheryl's story

Have you ever been at a crossroad in your life?

Do you go left, right or forward, or do you turn back to where you came from? But as Will Rogers once said, 'You can be on the right track but you'll get run over if you just sit there.'

On October 15th, 2011, you would have seen me sitting inside the Troxy Theatre, a large art deco building. It has two sweeping staircases that would have been perfect for the likes of Fred Astaire and Ginger Rogers, but it wasn't dancers that took to the stage that day – it was speakers.

'Who's this?' asked the Indian woman sitting next to me, and as I looked up at the stage, I could see the familiar face of a tall man with white hair. But this man is far from a pensioner – he's wearing an expensive blue suit and is dressed as if he is on his way to the office.

'Oh this is Bob Proctor – have you heard of him?'

Bob Proctor's voice echoes around the theatre: 'So many people tip-toe through life, trying to reach death safely. When I die, I want to be thoroughly used up.'

The audience is clapping and raising hands in agreement. I'm not sure if I'm in the right place, because this is a far cry from my everyday life …

Let me take you into my world.

My work days are long. I leave the house at 6 a.m. and return home 14 hours later. I often spend my days sitting in front of retail buyers who want to get everything at the cheapest price and they always want it yesterday. Today I am sitting opposite 'Dracula', a thin, pale, emotionless man, whose mantra is 'Work, work and more work.'

'Cheryl, I want to discuss something that happened when I was away. You didn't return my call last night for over 60 minutes. This is totally unacceptable.'

'But it was after 8 p.m. and I was out for dinner with some friends.'

'Cheryl, you should be on call 24/7. You get paid a salary, and get a company car and benefits. I will not tolerate this sort of behaviour – sort it out.'

I couldn't wait to get back to the sanctuary of my house and scream, 'It's not fair … I don't have a life!'

Back at the Troxy Theatre, the next speaker is announced: 'Ladies and gentlemen, please welcome to the stage Mr. Andy Harrington.'

I shrug at my neighbour – 'Never heard of this one' – but little did I know what was about to happen.

As Andy started his presentation, it was as if he was talking just to me: 'If you were to die tomorrow, who would mourn your loss?'

I remember thinking, 'Not a lot of people, because I never have time for anyone – I'm always working.'

Have you ever had a time when someone spoke to you and you had a connection, like they were on the same wavelength as you? That was what happened to me that day. How did he know what my life was like?

So when Andy presented the opportunity to attend the Public Speakers University, I ran to the back of the room. Not just for the course, which I really liked the sound of, but because I just knew Andy was going to help me. Don't ask me how I knew – I just did.

Work continued to be a nightmare: stressful, long hours, with no appreciation from Dracula. But after attending the Public Speakers University and being accepted as a member of the Professional Speakers Academy, I had found a new purpose in life and decided to work on Plan B, which was to set up my own business.

I'd love to tell you that it all went to plan but I found it increasingly impossible to live with a foot planted in two separate worlds. Dracula had sensed something was happening and interrogated me.

'Cheryl, it seems like this public speaking you've been doing is of more interest to you than your role here. You've got until this Friday to decide which is your priority?'

Have you ever known what you should do – what the right thing was to do, what every fibre of your body says you should do? Then your head says, 'You have a mortgage to pay. What about all the debt you have, Cheryl? You have responsibilities.'

I spent the next few days in turmoil. I couldn't speak to my family about it because I knew they would worry.

It was during that time that I got a call from my cousin Linda. 'Hey, Cheryl. Just checking that you're still coming over for Lynsey's birthday?'

'Hi, Linda. Yes, sorry I've not got back to you. I've had a lot on. Yeah, I'll be there. We'll have a good natter then, okay?'

This was not a usual 'birthday' celebration. Lynsey, my Kylie Minogue lookalike cousin, had died ten years previously at the tender age of 27 from a disease called cystic fibrosis and this was a 'birthday celebration' to remember her life.

Linda's call reminded me of a conversation with Lynsey just before she died. 'Cheryl, I know I'm not going to have a long life, but I'm going to make sure I live a full life. I'd rather have five minutes of wonderful than a lifetime of regret.' As I put down the phone to Linda, the decision was made. I resigned.

It was tough at first; I lost my salary overnight, my financial situation was challenging and my family thought I'd gone mad.

However, suddenly I had time – so I made an action plan, I studied NLP and life coaching, and after attending the Public Speakers University and being accepted into the Professional Speakers Academy, I started moving in the right direction.

I became an A.C.E. (Academy Coaching Executive) for Andy's Jet Set Speaker System and within nine months I became one of the top speaker coaches in the world.

Today I travel all over the world, sharing a message of hope and help to large groups of people. In the last nine months I have spoken in Australia, Malaysia, Singapore, South Africa, Europe and the USA. I also have my own business called The Law of Action. I use Andy's strategies and tactics to promote my products and services.

And now I have more money in the bank than I have ever had before, a brand new car and a house I love.

But more importantly than all of that I now do what I love with the people I love, and I get to make a difference in the lives of thousands of people. Life is great.

Cheryl Chapman starting her expert career.

Covert in qualified leads

So your potential client has watched your advert on YouTube and you've convinced them to click a link and go to your website. Now we have to convert them into a qualified lead. Specifically, we need to deliver on our promise by giving them an opportunity to receive some free training from us. In doing so, they will be giving their contact information so they can receive it from you.

Clearly, this means you need a website. But I want to be clear here – I am NOT talking about some corporate-looking website with a standard 'About us' page and all those navigational tabs that force visitors to hunt around for information.

Instead, you need what is commonly called an opt-in or squeeze-page website, where the only focus is to invite people to get your free training. Typically you'll need an opt-in video (which plays automatically as soon as they visit the site) and a place for people to enter their contact information so that they can get the free training.

Here's an example of our opt-in page.

To see this opt-in page live, simply visit ***www.jetsetspeaker.com***.

It's important to understand that just because people have navigated to your website from YouTube, Google or Facebook, it doesn't mean they will automatically sign up for your free training. The layout of the page makes a difference, but the most important thing to consider is the quality and structure of your opt-in video.

Getting the opt-in

First, you must have something that people really want. It doesn't matter how well you come across in the video if the free training doesn't hit all the right buttons. Your opt-in video must be relatively short – something like two minutes is ideal. In the video you must position yourself as an authority, promise to solve a problem they have relating to your topic, briefly talk about the free training or information and what they will get, and finally call them to action. You must be very specific about how they input their details in the boxes provided to get it.

All being well, you now have a new prospect on your list within your contact management system that will now be sent your free information or training. Now it's time to …

Campaign and sell

For your free training product to be effective, it must not only teach and demonstrate the quality of your information but it must also seed the idea that there are further advanced training sessions and products available. This is a crucial understanding because when you create your free product, you should design, develop and deliver it with this outcome in mind. This means you should not just take some random report or video and throw it up online for free. Instead, you must create your free product deliberately as the first step in a campaign to win a new customer.

The key here is this concept of a campaign. Far too many people in our industry try to market their products or events with a one-off email or advert. As already discussed, that simply won't work. In our industry, a good campaign is a strategic sequence of individual promotion pieces that educate your potential client, and build trust, credibility and authority, while creating enough desire that they want more from you and are willing to pay for it.

You could achieve this through a short series of videos that inform, inspire and influence your potential client over a few days. Each video needs to be created with the dual intention of educating people while moving them closer to being ready to make a buying decision.

A typical sequence might look something like this:

1. An opt-in video (day 1).

Paul Bates

2. An instructional content video (day 1).

Paul Bates

3. An instructional content video (day 3).

Jonathan Cole Photography

4 An online live master class with an offer built in at the end (day 5).

Paul Bates

5. A video detailing the exclusive offer (day 7).

6. A follow-up video calling people to action (day 8).

> To experience a campaign like the one shown here, visit
> **www.publicspeakersuniversity.com**.

A value-added campaign like the one shown in the previous few pages recognizes a truth that not everyone is ready to make a buying decision the very first time they hit your website. Instead, you are offering something valuable while capturing their contact information and building a relationship over a number of days. In doing so, you are establishing yourself in their mind as an expert but also moving them closer to the point that they are ready to buy.

It's also important to know that not everyone who goes through the campaign will buy. But remember: you are now positioned in their mind. If you now put them into a longer-term, value-based sequence when they *are* ready to buy – perhaps when a solution is both urgent and important – they will remember you and know exactly where to find you.

Collaborate and accelerate

Once you have established your automatic marketing machine and made profits by feeding the machine with online advertising, it's time to collaborate and accelerate. Armed with your conversion rates and statistics, I recommend you approach other information marketers and engage in a joint venture.

Essentially this involves another list owner sending an email to their own list recommending people should visit your website to get your free product. It is a very simple way of driving more people to visit your website and therefore feed your campaign. Provided you form a joint venture with information marketers who have a list of people who are potential high-probability clients for you, this can be a very lucrative opportunity for both of you.

Typically, the way to structure the deal is to offer them either 50 per cent of the revenue of the product or service you will ultimately sell during your campaign. Alternatively, if it is appropriate to do so, you could offer them a reciprocal arrangement where in a few weeks' time they could mail your list or indeed you could offer them to mail your list first on their behalf.

This is why I have stressed the importance here of first building your own list through online advertising. Once you have built your list, you will find it much easier to find joint venture partners because you will have proven results based on your campaigns. So you can make some good assumptions about how much their 50 per cent will be worth, based on the size of their list. Also they are much more likely to agree to a reciprocal email if you have a decent-sized list already.

Turn your customers into affiliates

An often overlooked strategy of marketing is to get your customers to recommend you. Your best customers could be incentivized to send out emails to their contacts or post on their social media profiles. In doing so they will also send people to your website and yet again you'll be kick-starting your marketing campaign with your free product or training

The deal will again typically be a 50 per cent cut of the revenue generated from sales made during the campaign.

In a nutshell

- *Don't use traditional media like newspapers and radio.*

- *Capture attention online and target your customers.*

- *Drive online traffic to your website.*

- *Give away a free information product to gain contact details.*

- *Make the free gift the first step in a multi-step campaign.*

- *Throughout the campaign, build trust, credibility and authority.*

- *Make an offer during the campaign for a high-value product or service.*

- *After the campaign, put non-buyers into a follow-up sequence.*

- *Accelerate your reach through joint ventures and affiliates.*

CHAPTER 8

PERFORMING LIKE A PROFESSIONAL

O f all the skills you could master as someone sharing your knowledge, knowhow and wisdom, surely the ability to speak confidently, congruently and conversationally to larger and larger groups of people would come top of the list.

Your ability to get your message across and then ultimately influence an audience will determine your ability to make BIG money and an even BIGGER difference in the lives of the people it reaches.

For many people, the idea of standing up in front of an audience – or for that matter, in front of a camera – sends them into a tailspin. The fear of public speaking is higher on their list of fears than dying! But when we think about this further it makes no sense, since we are speaking in public all the time and are able to do this with little to no fear at all. However, if you suddenly stand up and speak to an audience, that's when the nerves kick in.

First and foremost you will be a much better speaker when you have crafted world-class content, which is bang on the money for the audience you are speaking to. When you put together a presentation where the information is so good, and so valuable, that even if you were the worst presenter in the world, the audience will still be hanging on your every word.

In Chapter 5, 'Producing World-class Content', I stressed the importance of structuring your content around a solution framework that will become your own Unique Branded Solution. Your UBS gives you a sense of confidence, as it provides a structure without the need to use boring and unmemorable bullet points during your presentation. Your UBS also gives you a freedom of expression whilst keeping you on track, on topic and on time.

Earlier in this book I also spoke of the importance of sharing not just information in the form of facts or ideas but also for you to stand up and share what you believe. As people sharing knowledge and knowhow, we must also provide motivation so that we don't only inform but also transform.

I have also shared the need to design, develop and deliver great stories to deepen an audience's understanding of your material. Stimulating the right hemisphere of the brain will connect to a deeper truth and facilitate a change in beliefs, thoughts, feelings, decisions, actions and therefore results.

The hallmark of a true thought leader is the quality of their ideas, strategies and tactics. But if you are to make it really BIG you need to master the art of speaking, whether to a small group of people in a meeting, thousands of people at a conference, or direct to camera for your website videos as part of your value-based sequence marketing campaigns.

Getting in the zone

As a speaker you must develop the ability to manage your emotional state. Clearly this is important, so you want to come across as professional and measured in your approach. Without the charisma and confidence of a top-class performer, your audience might not believe in you and buy into your message.

However, there is an even more important reason why you must first manage your emotional state: it's because you want to be able to influence the emotional state of your audience!

You have no doubt heard about the concept of taking your audience on a journey. It's an emotional journey of the higher beats of personal power, confidence and inspiration to the lower vibes of the heart or an introspective, reflective note of the mind. (More about this later in this chapter.)

This brings me to a fundamental shift in perspective if you are to become a world-class presenter. Here it is …

'Focus on your audience while trusting your unconscious mind to deliver your content.'

This means getting into the performance zone, as all professionals, athletes and presenters must do to perform at their peak. All skill at the level of mastery is unconscious behaviour. Consider a competent typist. They no longer look at the keyboard; instead, they trust their unconscious mind rather than looking at each individual key.

If you drive a car, you should be able to drive without thinking about it and instead focus on the other cars on the road. When I was learning to drive I remember making the mistake of being overly concerned about being able to see the hood of my car from my seated position. However, now I am a more accomplished driver I no longer need to think about the car. Instead, I look ahead in peripheral vision and trust my positioning on the road.

Have you ever had to squeeze through a narrow gap whilst driving your car? If so, you'll know this is easier if you go into peripheral vision and trust yourself to navigate through the gap. What you don't want to do is overly focus on what you wish to avoid, as you are more likely to steer off-course and hit it.

Peripheral vision is the key to high performance. Top sportspeople and athletes understand this because their ability, once honed into a skillset, is stored in the unconscious mind. They understand the importance of trusting themselves in the key clutch moments of a game so that they can rise to the top.

Public speaking is exactly the same. You must internalize your content during its creation and then practice so it becomes second nature. But

Molly Burr

Peripheral vision (getting in the zone) is the key to high performance.

the moment you present live, you must not think about your message. Instead, you must become fully present for your audience and trust that your content will come through you.

By going into peripheral vision as you walk out on stage, you will be accessing your unconscious mind, where all of your content and your presentation skills will be stored. This allows your conscious mind the freedom to read the room and make small alterations to your performance, since each audience is different.

Debunking a myth

In my seminars and workshops I will often ask, 'What is the most valuable resource to human beings?' People will shout out answers like love, money or other people. But of course there is a much more valuable commodity, and that is oxygen. I don't know if you have thought about this before, but speaking involves breathing. Specifically, when you are speaking, you are only ever breathing out. Go ahead and try and speak whilst you breathe in. If you just did it, you looked and sounded weird!

Clearly, at some point, having spoken whilst breathing out, you'll need to breathe in again. There is a lot of nonsense spoken about breathing when it comes to public speaking. No doubt you will have heard people saying you must breathe from low down in the diaphragm, taking in big, deep breaths so that you can project your voice. Let me tell you, if you start taking deep breaths throughout your presentation, you're going to look even weirder than trying to speak as you breathe in.

When you read a passage of text in a book, it tells you where to breathe. A comma means you take a small pause (and therefore half a breath) and a period means you a take a longer pause (and therefore a full breath). So you only need to pause for long enough to get enough air to comfortably reach the next comma or full stop!

The rate and pace at which we breathe is so intrinsically linked to our state. When we are fearful, we take much shorter breaths. We also increase the levels of adrenaline in our bloodstream, readying us to fight or flight. But whilst it's important to breathe normally when speaking on stage, don't think about it – focusing on breathing will screw it up, because breathing is yet again an unconscious skill.

The answer is to simply to punctuate your message with pauses. In doing so, you will be regulating your breathing and, importantly, giving yourself an opportunity to lubricate your mouth, swallow and give yourself time to access your content.

Rookie speakers tend to have an irregular breathing pattern, which induces anxiety. They don't swallow enough, so their vocal cords become dry and stretched, which impairs performance and further increases the feeling of fear. Because the body is under stress, the brain looks for a cause and concludes that public speaking is the problem. And hey presto – you now have a fear about it.

However, the real fear is running out of oxygen, which is definitely something to be afraid of. But the truth is, there is plenty of oxygen available when presenting, you just need to insert punctuation so that you can have some …!

Pausing will also entirely stop you from inserting filler sounds or words like 'err', 'um', 'actually' and 'basically' when presenting. You'll have a more measured, relaxed and conversational style that allows your brain enough time to access your content.

Teaching should not be a one-way street

Pausing isn't just to give you time. Your audience also needs an opportunity to take in what you've said so they can make a picture in their mind, reflect upon your point, and – hopefully – relate it directly to their own situation. This in turn stimulates an internal dialogue where they evaluate your idea and make a decision about whether to implement your advice or not. A simple pause of two, three or four seconds is enough for this processing to take place. There will be key moments in your presentation where it will make sense to pause for longer – often, right after you have delivered a powerful impact line.

Don't be perfect, be authentic

In all the years I have been teaching presentation skills, it seems that one of the most challenging principles is to simply be you. Many speakers adopt an onstage persona that is different to how they are offstage. This persona is often one of feeling they need to be perfect and not make any mistakes. However, no one is perfect, and so it comes across as insincere and inauthentic. It's almost as if the presenter is wearing a suit of armour to protect their real self underneath. They want to protect themselves from attack, but when you wear a suit of armour and look unbelievably perfect, this is exactly when people will fire arrows at you to try to find the chink in your armour.

The easiest way to get the audience onside is to share a situation where you show you weren't perfect and learnt a valuable lesson. The story you share should ideally relate to the topic you are teaching, although some stories are generic enough to work in most contexts. The story I shared in this book about my first presentation, where I ended up with ink on my head, is an example of this type of situation. It tells the audience that you are far from perfect and instead you are someone who has learnt by doing.

Stand and deliver

It is often said that some people have the ability to really 'own the stage' when they make a presentation. But what does this mean? As audience members, we make judgments about the presenter based on how they sound and look. I will discuss later in this chapter the subject of sounding good, so let's turn our attention now to looking good onstage or onscreen. I'm not talking here about your choice of clothes – although this is important. I mean your physicality – specifically, your posture and your stance – because physicality plays a big part in people's perception of you.

Most people just don't stand well, and this is magnified when you get up in front of an audience. Men tend to stand with their feet wide in the cowboy-like pose, and women often stand with their weight on one foot with uneven hips. Neither of these are professional postures of someone who is a trusted authority figure.

At the Public Speakers University, we teach speakers to stand confidently by having their feet hip-width apart with their pelvis in a neutral position and a nice lengthened spine. It isn't about being tall, but it is about using all your available height and being comfortable in your own skin.

> *To give you a visual reference for this technique and to watch me coach a member of an audience in how to improve their stage presence, I recorded a video for you. You can access it at **www.passionintoprofit.info**, under the heading entitled 'Stance'.*

Connection and rapport

As I have shared earlier in this book, your job as a speaker is not just to inform, but also to transform. In Chapter 5, 'Producing World-class Content', I discussed with you how to put your content together so that it facilitates this transformation. But a huge part of your ability to deliver that transformation will be shaped by the way in which you connect with your audience.

If there were just one presentation skill I would encourage you to master, it would be your eye contact. Most speakers have aerosol eyes, meaning they spray their eye contact all over the audience. This is a huge mistake because fleeting eye contact is normally a behaviour displayed by people who are untrustworthy.

Speak to all but look to one

Instead of a scattergun approach use a laser-like technique where you look directly at just one person whilst you deliver a sentence or thought. Then, once you reach a comma or period, radically shift your eye contact to someone else in the audience. Holding your eye contact with each member of your audience lets them know they are important and significant.

The shift of your eye contact should always be radical and not linear, as you don't want it to look like a deliberate technique. When you have a big audience, make your eye contact shifts even more radical, since there will be so many more people to get to. If you present in giant arenas as I often do, note each section of seating and make sure you connect with people in the front, middle and rear of each section. Because people are further away when you look at one person, 50–100 people will think you are looking directly at them.

Visit **www.passionintoprofit.info** and watch a video where you can see the power of using eye contact to connect with your audience. You'll find it under the heading 'Eye contact'.

As thought leaders we can do so much more than simply teaching. We have the opportunity to create real and lasting change. But it's a sad fact that many people hear great advice on how to improve their situation but fail to act, and fail to implement.

Why is that?

Often people are shut down to new ways of thinking and new paradigms that could be game-changers for them. I believe that our job as agents of change is to:

- Open people up where they were previously blocked

- Give them access to the awesome inner power within us all to turn any situation around

- Ignite their faith and belief in themselves to do anything they put their mind to.

Taking the audience on a journey

The true hallmark of a great speaker is their ability to take us on a journey. But what does this mean? The 'journey', as we call it, is a rollercoaster ride of emotions the audience experience throughout your speech. But to do so we must be willing to ride the rollercoaster with them.

In a few moments I will introduce you to four archetypes living with you. An archetype is the notion that we all have different characters, or parts of ourselves we can call upon in any given situation. These archetypes are not real; they exist as metaphorical characters, giving us quick and easy access to an emotional state more appropriate to the situation at hand.

Interestingly, having worked with many thousands of people, I've found that not everyone is comfortable expressing themselves through each of these three archetypes. Often this is because of events in their past that have caused them to reject, or 'cover over', certain archetypes. This can also result in the overuse of one specific archetype so that it becomes too dominant, making people too 'one-dimensional' and therefore less effective.

When we are in rapport with our audience and then slip into expressing our message through these archetypes, we shift the mood in the room. By doing so, you'll be awakening dormant archetypes for people that may just be the key to unlocking their ability to understand, implement and get ahead.

Although there are many more archetypes, let's take a look at the four main ones.

1. The Sage

The Sage within us is on a quest to discover hidden truths. It is said that knowledge is power, but the Sage is instead on a hunt for wisdom. The Sage is not afraid to share their power. Where some think, 'If I share my power, I lose my power,' the Sage comes from a place of abundance that says, 'If I share my power, I increase my power.'

The Sage communicates in a clear and resonate tonality. They never rush their words; their speech is deliberate and meaningful. The volume and pace of their speech is right in the middle of their range, but it is far from monotone. In fact, their voice is melodic and rhythmic, and somewhat hypnotic to all those tuned into it.

2. The Warrior

The Warrior within us is courageous and determined to fight for what is right. Not in a physical sense, but in the energy of their conviction and commitment to do what is necessary to do the job.

The Warrior sets the boundaries of our kingdom and the standard for our own behaviour and those people in our inner circle. The Warrior is not afraid to be different when they need to be – they can say no and be okay with it.

The Warrior within us wants to explore new horizons and broaden the boundaries of the kingdom in search of new experiences and new adventures.

The Warrior speaks and moves with certainty, with a voice that is direct and authoritative. They mean what they say and say what they mean. They call people to action and influence people to march forth and become leaders in their own right. Their words are louder, shorter and punchy, and have an immediate impact that makes their troops feel motivated and ready for action.

3. The Lover

The Lover within us is open, trusting and vulnerable. I'm not talking about the kind of vulnerability that says 'I am weak and broken.' Instead, I mean a vulnerability that demonstrates a level of authenticity, transparency and genuineness that comes from the centre of who you really are.

The Lover within you brings people together and shares from the heart, speaking softly, with much longer pauses, allowing people to feel the impact of your message through an inward reflection. The resonance of the Lover's voice has a vibration of love not often heard in public.

4. The Jester

In days gone by, the courts of kings and queens would employ the services of a jester to amuse and entertain their guests. Interestingly, the jester would also make fun of the king or queen in a way no one else would be permitted to do.

The job of your Jester when onstage is to burst your own ego and not take yourself too seriously. Your Jester is spontaneous and fast-thinking, with wit and humour. Even though a Jester is self-deprecating, it is always done with a feeling of 'I'm okay with who I really am.' Most importantly, the Jester affords people the chance to relax and enjoy themselves whilst learning valuable lessons through your presentation. The Jester expresses themselves in a higher-pitch tone, with short and explosive bursts of words, often in a flippant or unexpected way that catches people off-guard, prompting laughter.

Match the mood

The key to taking the audience on a journey is to flow in and out of the different energies of these archetypes, sometimes even in one single sentence. Clearly, some moments of your message lend themselves better to one archetype more than another. Knowing this, you can begin to deliberately influence the audience's state so that your message is absorbed at the unconscious level.

Each of these archetypes can be enhanced with a gesture that helps you to express them when speaking and anchors the audience into accessing them. Gestures are a visual representation of your emotions, so it should feel natural to express yourself with each one if you are communicating from the appropriate archetype.

Earlier on in this chapter we talked about having a good stance in order to have presence. But to truly 'own the stage', you must also move with purpose too. Many rookie speakers wander aimlessly around the stage or, conversely, stay rooted to one spot. By walking purposely to the flanks and staying there for a while, you demonstrate your willingness to connect with everyone, not just those people at the front and centre.

Lizzie Ayton

The Sage (measured and considered).

The Warrior (punchy and direct).

The Lover (open, vulnerable and trusting).

Gagan Arora

Acting the fool as the Jester (asymmetrical).

Before you walk to a new place on the stage, lock eyes with a member of the audience who is in the direction you are moving. This gives you a focus and intention to move and will look totally natural.

If you want to 'move people' with your message, you'll need to move around the stage. But don't pace up and down, or you'll look like a caged tiger looking to escape! Always pause when you get to where you're going and communicate from that spot for a while. Sometimes you can even move out into the audience to share your message more intimately and conversationally. Tony Robbins is particularly adept at doing this, but at 6 feet 7 inches tall, he probably doesn't need the stage as much as I do …!

Getting offstage and among the audience to create intimacy.

Getting to the flanks to connect with people on the sides of the audience.

In a nutshell

- *Punctuate your message with pauses.*

- *Let go of your content, trust it will be there and get in the zone.*

- *Be yourself, as everyone else is taken ...!*

- *Develop your stage presence by standing in your power.*

- *Take the audience on a journey of emotions.*

- *Access your archetypes and open up your audience.*

- *Let your gestures be a natural expression of how you feel.*

- *Move with purpose and own the stage.*

CHAPTER 9

PERSUADING PEOPLE TO BUY

Here's an interesting question. What do all successful businesses have in common? The answer is they all sell something for a profit. This book is entitled *Passion into Profit*, and for you to make those profits, people need to buy your information products, seminars, workshops, webinars and mastermind programmes. If you haven't produced something to sell yet, then re-read Chapter 5, 'Creating Word-class Content' and Chapter 6, 'Productizing Your Knowledge', and get producing and publishing something to sell. Don't worry if your first attempt doesn't produce something amazing. Trust me – you'll get better.

Okay, time for a rant.

If there's one thing that drives me crazy, it's the notion that selling is bad. Selling is good – well, the kind of selling I will reveal here, anyway. Remember a product or service you provide essentially solves a problem for your clients or enhances their quality of life. So why would you feel bad about helping someone?

Before money was invented, people would exchange their services or barter with each other. This meant the more you did for others, the more favours you stacked up, so that if you needed something done you could call in the favour. But today it is money that stacks up in our bank account, not favours. Simply put, the more money you have, the more people you have helped! This means that those without enough money have not yet found an effective way of helping lots of people.

Pitching to large groups of people

So how do you help lots of people and be handsomely rewarded for your efforts? The answer is to pitch your products and services to large groups of people all at once. Think about it: why would you sell one-to-one when you can sell one-to-many?

Here are the three primary ways to pitch to large groups of people:

1. An offer made through an online webinar

A webinar is an online seminar. Essentially, registrants to the webinar are sent a unique link via email. When they click the link they are taken to the webinar, which enables them see what your computer is displaying and hear your voice live.

To host a webinar, all you'll need are your PowerPoint or Keynote slides and a computer with a microphone (which is normally built in). You will also need a webinar provider. The most commonly used is GoToWebinar and is very easy to use.

The benefits of using a webinar is that it's relatively inexpensive, as you won't have to hire a venue and pay for a sound technician and AV. Also, if you put on a live event and hire a venue and only ten people show up when the room holds 100, it won't look too good. With an online webinar, the participants can't see how many people are on the webinar – only you can!

Webinars are typically 60–90 minutes in length, which is enough time to deliver a great presentation and a well-crafted pitch. The downside of a webinar compared to a live event is that you may find your conversion drops the higher the price point, as there isn't quite as much trust generated.

2. An offer made through a recorded online video

In Chapter 7, 'Promoting Your Products and Services', I outlined a campaign where your potential customer opts in and receives two or three training videos followed by an offer video, where you sell a product or service. This strategy is particularly useful if you are selling a slightly higher priced product or seminar, as you will have created more trust, credibility and authority over the course of the campaign. For the video to be effective, you'll need to spend more money to produce.

3. An offer made during a live seminar

This can either be a free or low-paid preview event that you have marketed, or it could be an event that you have been invited to be a guest speaker at. Either way you'll be presenting for approximately 60–90 minutes and making your offer during your presentation for people to purchase your products or services right there and then in the room. The advantage of a live event is that your conversions will typically be the highest of all three options and the order transaction value will also be the highest too.

The downside is it's harder to market people to come to a live event (even if it's free), as they have to travel and be available to attend. Also, for every 100 people who register for the live event, only around 30 to maybe 40 people will attend. In addition, there is the increased cost of putting on the event.

A strategy that works the best is a webinar or sales video where you offer people an entry-level product or service and then upsell them on coming to a live event. This way, the attendance will be almost 100 per cent, because people have paid to attend and have more to lose if they don't show. During your paid event you will also be able to make an offer for an even higher value product or service.

Present, pitch and grow rich

Regardless of your mode of delivery, there are certain principles you must follow when creating and delivering this type of presentation.

In Chapter 7, 'Promoting Yourself and Your Services', I introduced the principle of 'give first before you receive'. When it comes to selling on a webinar, online video or live on a stage, this means that teaching and educating is the premise for the presentation. However, there is an art and a science regarding what information to include or leave for another time.

When it comes to a short presentation with a pitch, the biggest mistake that experts make is to drill down too deep into their content. If you do this in a short presentation, you will usually overwhelm or confuse people – and confused people do not buy. To really understand the nuances of how to do something, people need to experience it, get their hands on it and ask questions. This all takes time and it's time you don't have in a short presentation.

The second mistake that experts make is to teach content all the way through their presentation and then bolt a pitch on the end. This simply will not work. When you spring an offer on your audience at the end, they haven't had enough thinking time to run their buying strategy and decide if they want it or not. I'm not saying you won't make sales – the impulsive people and those who are at the right stage of the buying cycle might buy, but this isn't going to be a high percentage of people.

The third mistake is in not having an irresistible offer to buy on the day. The offer must be so good that people feel compelled to buy because the deal is structured into a special package offered only to those who buy within a certain time period (usually on the day). Trust me, if you give people the option to put off a decision and get back to you another day, most likely you will never hear from them again.

Use your solution framework

In Chapter 5, 'Producing World-class Content', I extolled the virtues of having a UBS. Creating a presentation around your UBS allows you to keep the majority of your content at the conceptual and theoretical level without making the mistake of going too deep.

First, your presentation should start with a goal or aspiration that you are certain your audience want. Then it should move on to the problems and challenges they face in achieving it. This immediately creates a gap between where they are and where they want to be, and makes clear the obstacles that they will need to overcome to get there.

Second, introduce your solution framework or UBS as something that will overcome the challenges and obstacles ahead. Each part of your solution should solve a specific problem that your audience have (or will have) in the pursuit of their goal.

Take a look at the Jet Set Speaker System for a visual representation of my UBS for teaching my audiences how to become a world-class speaker.

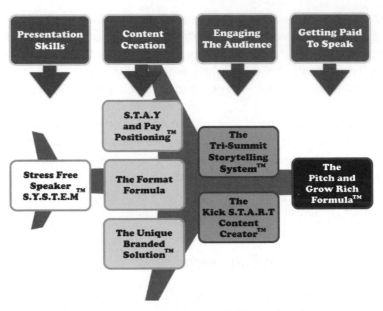

The Jet Set Speaker System and all its subsystems

The top four boxes relate to the problems (or areas to be addressed) and below are the individual systems to resolve these issues.

Your solution framework becomes a map that guides the audience in how to get from where they are to where they want to be, and it's the information contained in the layers below the overall framework they will be buying.

The key in the early part of your presentation is the positioning of *your* UBS as the solution to your audience's problems. Under each of the systems shown in the Jet Set Speaker System are step-by-step instructions and specific tactics to achieve success and solve each of the problems they relate to.

After positioning your UBS, it's time to get under the hood by choosing just one of your sub-systems and revealing some of the strategies, tactics and steps underneath. In doing so you'll be demonstrating the depth and quality of your solution framework, but – crucially – without revealing it all.

It's important to remember that we don't want to go too deep and reveal everything during this presentation, as we will overwhelm and confuse our audience. In any event, there won't be enough time in a short presentation anyway.

*For an example of a webinar presentation where I make a pitch for one of my products, visit **www.jetsetspeaker.com**.*

Structuring your talk this way highlights the problems to be solved and the obstacles to overcome whilst informing your audience WHAT they need to focus on to solve it (through the overview of your UBS). You will have also given them an insight into HOW to solve one of the problems (through diving deeper into one of your subsystems).

Incompletion is the key

By presenting your content in this way, your audience will experience a sense of incompletion. You've shown them the map of the whole solution and given them a taste of what's underneath. At the end of your presentation they will know how good your information is and now they want more, and this of course is what you'll offer them. You'll be selling a solution where they either learn all of it in longer, more advanced training or a 'done for you' service where you implement the system for them, or perhaps a product that automates the whole process.

This feeling of incompletion is an important one to create for your audience. They will now be aware there is a gap between where they are and where you can take them which needs to be closed, and they know your product or service will do the job!

> **'Selling is making people aware of a gap between where they are and where they want to be. Your solution is the bridge to overcome this gap.'**

At some point in the presentation your audience are going to be hungry for the total solution and will want to hear what is on offer to get it. What most speakers do is wait until the very end of their presentation before making an offer. This is a BIG mistake.

The Jet Set Speaker System is my solution to help people overcome the problems lurking in the water.

Your audience need time to run their buying strategy and convince themselves they want what you have and can justify the purchase. So instead of waiting until the end, first casually mention the name of your product or service when you introduce your UBS for the first time. Then drop it into your talk a few more times, but without selling it – just mentioning it. I might say:

> 'At the Public Speakers University, I teach people how to perform at their peak every time they speak, and I do that by teaching them the Stress Free Speaker System, because most people don't find it easy to speak in front of a group of people and deliver a message with certainty, confidence and congruency. But why is that? Well …'

You can see from the snippet above that the audience are now aware of the Public Speakers University and that people are getting great results from attending. This is designed to be very casual, and is mentioned as part of the content rather than a direct pitch, thus unconsciously increasing curiosity and desire.

The showcase

Next, at a point approximately halfway to two-thirds of the way through your presentation, I suggest you deliberately and confidently make a pitch. I call this the showcase. This is where you showcase your product or service, and explain what it is, how it works, who it's for (and who it's not for), why it's unique, what the benefits are and the results it can produce, plus all the logistical details, including price.

Price itself is very important. You must never introduce the price without first building value – and, more specifically, proof of value. It's all very well you telling people it's the best thing since sliced bread, but it's a whole different matter when someone else does. If at all possible, get an authority figure or a celebrity to endorse your product or service, as their words will carry more weight with your audience.

Once you have completed your showcase, just roll straight back into your presentation without closing (you will do this at the end). By going straight on with your talk, you allow time for your audience to start thinking about whether they want what you have to offer. Whilst you continue with your message, their buying strategy is running in the background. From here on, your content can serve to convince them further they should buy.

The call to action

This structure means that all of the selling has already been done way before the end of your talk, which means by this point that many people are ready to buy. However, to get an even higher conversion, it makes sense to sweeten the deal a little and either give a discount on the price, or include some bonus products if they make a commitment on the day (or within a certain time period). Be sure to make the offer very clear and then be very direct in the action you want the audience to take, so there is no misunderstanding of what they need to do to take up the offer.

Remember the buying experience should be exciting and fun: for you, because you are making money while making a difference, and for your customers because they are stepping up to the next level.

The industry has changed

For quite some time, too many speakers gave empty content without any real useful value. Their presentations were just a series of stories about themselves and showing pictures of their achievements, but there was no actionable content being shared. I believe the days of this style of presentation are over and we must get back to delivering value in all of our presentations, whether we are selling or not. Remember as long as you have created a world-class product or service and structured your presentation as I have suggested, you will be giving great value.

I also believe you should work to improve the overall quality of your products and services. Take great pride in the impact of each part of the customer experience from your office staff to your emails, your website, your keynote slides, your manuals, name badges and certificates, etc., and look to consistently improve them over time.

Above all else, be proud of what you do and make no apologies for making an offer. Remember, selling is about solving people's problems – so get out there and help others and you will be well rewarded.

In a nutshell

- *Selling is good.*

- *Your products and services solve real problems, so be proud to sell.*

- *Choose webinar, online video or live event as your medium of selling.*

- *Create your presentation around your UBS.*

- *Generate a feeling of incompletion so that the audience buy to get completion.*

- *Your solution must bridge the gap between where the audience currently are and where they want to be.*

- *Showcase your product or service well before the end.*

- *Sweeten the deal and incentivize people to buy now.*

CHAPTER 10

POWERING UP YOUR PERSONALITY

I very much hope this book has been a reawakening for you. I hope it has helped you to see the huge potential you have to help others and make money. But I also expect you have doubts about your ability and fears about whether anyone would listen or take your advice, let alone pay for it! Please know these feelings are normal and natural.

When you arrived in the world you were brilliant, amazing, like a sparkling diamond, unique, special, one of a kind, outstanding and individual. However, I suspect as you grew up, you experienced that society didn't support you in standing out, trusting your voice and expressing your opinions.

As a result, perhaps like many people, you learned to cover over your uniqueness, mute your voice and your opinions, and instead shrink down to fit in. Effectively putting a protective layer on top of your diamond. Perhaps you also encountered difficult events in your life and perhaps as a result you added even more layers. These layers come in the forms of fears, disempowering beliefs and self-imposed limitations.

You are not alone. Many of us have believed these protective layers were real and forgotten we are that brilliant sparkling diamond, with unique talents and abilities, and the power to create the life we deserve.

This book has given you many new tools, strategies and techniques to shine your light and make your difference in the world. However there is a danger you may never formulate your message, implement the ideas shared in this book and promote yourself if you don't believe you can. This is why I have saved this short chapter on personal empowerment until last so you complete this book ready to make a difference and leave a legacy.

Get creative, get playful

Was there a time in your life where you felt more free and abundant than you do now? For most of us that was early on in life when we were kids, before we had our childhood conditioned out of us.

Are kids naturally spontaneous? Are they loving and warm towards strangers? Are they natural communicators? Are they learning sponges? Is their primary focus to have fun? Are they okay with being emotional? Do they wake up in the morning with bundles of energy and a big happy smile on their face?

Look at someone like Richard Branson. Is he playful? Does he like having fun? Is he warm and friendly, even towards strangers? Does he take risks? Does he dare to dream? Are his businesses constantly growing and expanding? Is he okay with making fun of himself? Is he spontaneous? And his brand name Virgin tells you everything about him.

What happened to us? That childlike state is our natural state. Think about it: how much attention does a child of say five, six or seven give to what happened three or four weeks ago? How much attention do they give to what might happen in three to four weeks' time? Not a whole lot, is it? So where does a child of that age range live, then? That's right – the present moment. NOW is where they live.

Time to return home

What about most adults? Where do they live? Some get stuck in the past, some constantly hang out in the future. But the one place most adults don't live consistently is right now, the present moment. How come? How can it be that we were once fully in the moment, living in our essence, living in our heart and our soul, and yet somehow we moved away from home? And now we live in our heads.

For me the answer is simple. In the stillness of the present moment there is often a message that requires us to take an action we are afraid to take and to step up to bigger things. Instead, we keep ourselves busy and live in the dimension of distraction, doing things we believe are urgent while rarely doing those things that are important.

If you are going to truly serve with your message, you must drill down to find your diamond and remove any protective layers that stop you from committing to becoming a source of information and inspiration to others. For only when you are authentically moving forward and taking new bolder action in pursuit of your dreams will you build a momentum towards real and lasting success.

If you want to be a *New York Times* bestseller, speak in giant arenas all over the world and pull in millions in revenue for your business, clearly what's required are different beliefs about your ability, new empowering habits and bigger and bolder actions.

So the big question is how do we get ourselves from where we are right now to where we want to be?

Molly Burr

What got you here won't get you there

First and foremost you must be willing to leave behind where you are right now. You must give up old actions, beliefs, values and excuses that you've been hanging onto as you start out on your journey.

As you step into the unknown you may feel exposed, uncomfortable, confused and potentially vulnerable. When this happens you may want to turn around and run back to what you know and forget all about your dreams.

Most people run back to the comfort and safety of what they know even though it ultimately makes them feel dead inside. When they arrive

Molly Burr

In stepping up we often feel exposed and vulnerable and want to run back to the relative comfort of our office desk.

back they immediately begin to justify their behaviour by saying to themselves things like 'I didn't want it anyway', or 'Who did I think I was to have these big dreams and plans? I know my place, I know where I fit in', or 'All those people who said I couldn't do it, that I mustn't do it, that I shouldn't do it – I guess they were right.'

When we feel the voices of self-doubt creeping in, we must interrupt them so that we stay focused on our mission and our goals. But how do you do that? It turns out it's a lot simpler than you might think.

When we talk to ourselves, we are often making statements that are expressed as beliefs such as follows:

- 'If I do X, then Y will happen.'

- 'I can't do it.'

- 'I am no good.'

- 'There's just no way I'll ever be able to do it …'

- 'I'm just not good enough.'

- 'I'll never be as good as …'

Whenever we say things like 'There's just no way I'll ever be able to do it', we begin to shut down and become demotivated. These statements act as circuit breakers that stop us from moving forwards and make us want to return back to our comfort zone.

In our moments of self-doubt we might also be asking ourselves poor-quality questions such as 'Why doesn't it ever seem to work for me?' or 'Why am I so stupid?' or 'What is wrong with me?' or 'How come I never finish what I start?'

Think of your mind as a search engine, and the questions you ask are the search terms used. When you type a question into Google, it will give you a series of results that best match the question. So when in a moment of self-doubt you say, for example, 'Why am I so stupid?' your mind will search for all the times in the past where you made a mistake and deliver them to the forefront of your mind, just as Google would do.

As you can imagine, this kind of negative self-talk will only serve to increase feelings of inadequacy and cause us to feel fearful while becoming stuck. Some people advocate techniques to attempt to turn off this voice, but I believe it makes more sense to simply change what it's saying. We need a series of new statements about our abilities and our identity, and

POWERING UP YOUR PERSONALITY

also a set of new, empowering questions that change our focus in those key moments.

Here are a few you might find helpful.

New statements

- 'If I take action, I will either win or I will learn something … and I love learning.'

- 'When information runs out, it's time for me to make a decision.'

- 'I can achieve anything I put my mind to.'

- 'I can break down any complex task into smaller tasks so it becomes easy for me to achieve.'

- 'I am good with people.'

- 'I am good with numbers.'

- 'I am good with money.'

- 'I am good with technology.'

- 'I am a leader.'

- 'If someone else can do it, I can do it too.'

- 'I am guided.'

- 'Everything happens for a reason that supports my journey.'

New questions

- 'What can I learn from this?'

- 'What is good about this situation?'

- 'How can I reach even more people with my message?'

- 'Who already knows how to do this?'

- 'How can I double my results?'

- 'What am I excited about today?'

- 'What am I passionate about today?'

- 'What is the one thing I can do today to move me closest to my goal?'

A good coach or consultant asks great questions to facilitate a change in thinking. On your journey to success you need to become your own best coach and consultant. Questions change what you focus on, so it makes sense to ask those questions that cause you to focus on the things that help you tap into your power to achieve.

It is inevitable that you will at times feel uncertain, and for your motivation levels to wane. However, by adding your own questions to those above and conditioning yourself to ask them in those key moments, you'll be directing your mind to find the answers that will keep you on the right track.

"

The road to success has many tempting parking spaces.

Will Rogers

"

Next steps

If you are like most people, you will have read this book without yet putting into action the steps to build a success business in this industry. So with this in mind, here's your action plan.

Position yourself as an expert authority

- Decide who you will serve.

- Emphasize what makes you unique.

- Put a stake in the ground and claim your subject.

- Position yourself as the 'go to guru' for your audience.

Prove your credibility with a personal story

- Craft a personal story to position yourself as a trusted source of information.

- Your story should also provide a valuable lesson.

- Stories must not be told – they must be relived.

- Centre a story on a challenge you overcame to become who you are.

- Tell your story mostly through dialogue, not narration.

Produce world-class content

- Produce a solution framework for your ideas.

- Brand your solution by giving it a unique and catchy name.

- Don't just inform people – transform them too.

- Be controversial, be different and attack the status quo.

- Associate your points with things that people are already familiar with.

Productize your knowledge

- Package your knowledge and knowhow to grow your business.

- Create information products so you can reach your audience more easily.

- People may want to read, hear, watch or experience your content.

- Charge a premium for one-to-one sessions with you.

Promote yourself and your services

- Capture attention online and target your customers.

- Drive online traffic to your website.

- Give away a free information product to gain contact details.

- Make the free gift the first step in a multistep campaign.

- Build trust credibility and authority through the campaign.

- Make an offer during the campaign for a high-value product or service.

- After the campaign, put non-buyers into a follow-up sequence.

- Accelerate your reach through joint ventures and affiliates.

Perform like a professional

- Punctuate your message with pauses.

- Let go of your content and trust it will be there, and get in the zone.

- Be yourself, as everyone else is taken …!

- Develop your stage presence by standing in your power.

- Take the audience on a journey of emotions.

- Access your archetypes and open up your audience.

- Let your gestures be a natural expression of how you feel.

- Move with purpose and own the stage.

Persuade people to buy

- Choose a webinar, online video or live event as your medium of selling.

- Create your presentation around your UBS.

- Generate a feeling of incompletion so that the audience buys to get completion.

- Bridge the gap between where the audience are and where they want to be with your solution.

- Showcase your product or service well before the end of your presentation.

- Sweeten the deal and incentivize people to buy now.

Power up your personality

- Live in the now.

- Generate powerful statements about your identity and ability.

- Create and use new, empowering questions to keep you focused.

I hope that reading *Passion into Profit* has inspired you to share the valuable lessons you have acquired on your journey and to believe in your voice as a source of hope, help and inspiration to others.

I believe by expressing our ideas and standing up for what we believe in, we come to know ourselves and, in doing so, define the mission of why we are here. I have come to understand that for all the wisdom or knowledge I share with others, I need to always be listening to my own advice and be certain that I am being true to myself.

Above all else, I wish for you to that you are guided and have been shaped and sculpted your whole life to be the unique and talented soul you were destined to be. Now it's time to recognize your huge potential to help others. Pass on your knowhow, share your knowledge and in the process you will be rewarded financially and more importantly with a sense of fulfillment from making a difference.

If I can be of further assistance to you through my products and live courses, I would be deeply honoured to be able to serve you once again. I look forward to meeting you and hearing about your successes in person. Until then, I wish you all the health, wealth and happiness in the world.

Andy x

ABOUT
ANDY HARRINGTON

Andy Harrington is the founder of The Professional Speakers Academy an exclusive incubator for producing world-class speaking talent.

He is also the creator of The Public Speakers University where coaches, consultants, authors, practitioners, therapists, entrepreneurs, salespeople, trainers, managers, and those with the desire to share a message of hope and help, learn how to design, develop and deliver outstanding presentations on stage or through on-line video.

Andy also created the Power to Achieve Weekend Event which has helped thousands of people to break through self-imposed limitations and create the life they deserve.

Andy Harrington's training programs have been delivered in the United Kingdom, USA, Canada, Australia, New Zealand, South Africa, UAE, Ireland, Holland, Belgium, Poland, Germany, Slovenia, Switzerland, Singapore, Malaysia and Thailand.

He has shared the stage with presidents, business leaders and advice guru's such as Sir Richard Branson, Bill Clinton, Donald Trump, Alan Sugar, Sir Bob Geldof, Steve Wozniak, Tony Robbins, Robert Kiyosaki, Brian Tracy, Bob Proctor as well as other leaders in the mentoring industry.

Meet Andy and receive your free world-class training at
AndyHarrington.com

ACKNOWLEDGEMENTS

I would not be the person I am today (and therefore this book would never have been written) without the love, support and influence of many people.

To my beautiful wife Beckie, you are my soul mate and the wind beneath my wings. I am so grateful for the tireless work and gentle caring you give to all of us. You are a true diamond and I am so happy to have discovered you. I will treasure you forever.

To my Mum and most avid supporter, thank you is not enough to describe the caring you have shown me throughout our lives. Thank you for showing me the meaning of unconditional love.

To my Dad, for the formative years of my life and shaping me to achieve. Thank you for all those years standing on the sidelines and watching me play football. And to my big sister Una, for always being there, just in case.

To my children Josh, Tom, Gemma, Amelia and Alfie, all so unique and amazing. I'm proud to be your Dad. You bring joy and purpose to my life. Thank you for being my reason to strive and be alive.

To Peter, Caroline, Sarah and Lizzy, thank you for welcoming me into your family and making me feel at home and for the crazy parties …!

To Tony Robbins, you awakened the giant within. Without you, this book would never have been written.

ACKNOWLEDGEMENTS

Thank you to Richard Tan, Veronica Chew, Michael Burnett and Michael Lane for your support in helping me to reach a wider audience around the world through your amazing events.

To all those that blazed a trail for me to follow: Greg Secker, Brian Tracy, Bob Proctor, Stephen Covey, Jack Canfield, Darren Winters, Mark Victor Hansen, Robert Kiyosaki, T. Harv Eker, Wayne Dyer, Les Brown, Brendon Burchard, Denis Waitley, Joseph McClendon III, Peter Sage and David Shephard of the Performance Partnership.

To all the incredible marketing geniuses who have helped me reach out online to help even more people: Frank Kern, Ryan Deiss, Jeff Walker, Eben Pagan, Jeff Johnson, Mike Koenigs, Yanik Silver, Chris Cardell, Mike Filsaime, Andy Jenkins, Armand Morin and Jo Polish.

Thanks to Andrew Reynolds for taking a gamble on me and putting me on stage at Entrepreneurs Bootcamp. To Simon Coulson for your friendship and sound marketing advice. To Shaa Wasmund for introducing me to my publisher, Wiley and to Holly Bennion for believing in me.

I am very grateful to the amazing team at AndyHarrington.com, including Mat Wilson, marketing extraordinaire, and his team Ludovic Stephenson, Max Lammas, Craig Wilson and Josh Harrington. To Andy Fairbairns for being my left brain and the rest of the admin team of Chloe and Loraine Borowczyk, Jo Webb and Janeille Griffiths.

Thank you also to the ACE team of incredible mentors who teach, train and support the many members of the Professional Speakers Academy around the world. A special thank you to Cheryl Chapman, chief engineer of the Jet Set Speaker System. Thanks also to the army of volunteers who work tirelessly at my live events and act as an example of what is possible to our customers.

ACKNOWLEDGEMENTS

It's impossible to thank everyone who has supported me on my journey, but please know I am forever grateful to all my customers, partners, friends and family.

One final and perhaps unexpected thank you goes to my old English teacher, Mr Dyke, at Longfield Comprehensive School in Kent. For reasons unbeknown to me he once proclaimed to the entire class I was a genius. To this day I still do not know why he did it. Truth is, I was never that good at English – my spelling, grammar and punctuation always let down my creative side.

However, he believed in me, which brings me to my final point. We may never know the full impact of what we do or say to inspire others. The rippling effect may continue for many years and be passed on from generation to generation – so go forth and make waves.

> **"There are people in the world, who are willing to pay good money, to know what you already know."**

Being a great speaker has been a Hallmark of quality individuals for thousands of years, and today it is more important than ever.

The Public Speakers University will transform you into a master speaker by gaining these prized speaking techniques:

Impact - Discover how to generate a powerful presence whilst remaining totally comfortable, confident and congruent on stage and on video, so you perform at your peak every time you speak.

Inform – Become an instant authority with your own custom designed unique branded solution. Enjoy the freedom of personal expression coupled with the precision to stay on task, on topic and on time.

Inspire – Learn how to take your audience on an epic adventure without leaving the room as you cleverly weave subtle messages into anecdotal stories that speak a deeper truth and lift our spirit.

Influence – Realise your ability to become an agent of change and revolutionise how you create and deliver content forever. Go beyond simply delivering information and discover the secrets to facilitating a real and lasting transformation for your audiences around the world.

Income – Acquire the ability to package your knowledge into irresistible offers for high-end products and programs people are so excited to own and experience they literally run to the back of the room to buy from you before you've even finished your presentation!

> **"Educate your target market, and you'll be increasing your power, positioning and price, whilst becoming the go to expert for your industry."**

www.andyharrington.com

Andy Harrington's **Public Speakers University**

Andy Harrington
The World's Leading Public Speaking Expert